D0426301

The Little Book of
GOLF
LEGENDS

This edition first published in the UK in 2006
By Green Umbrella

© Green Umbrella Publishing 2008

www.gupublishing.co.uk

Publishers Jules Gammond and Vanessa Gardner

Printed and bound in Italy

ISBN 978-1-905009-55-8

CONTENTS

CONTENTS

SEVERIANO
BALLESTEROS

Born: Pedrena, Spain April 9, 1957
Turned Professional: 1974
Masters: Winner in 1980, 1983
US Open: 3rd in 1987
Open: Winner in 1979, 1984, 1988
USPGA: 5th in 1984
Ryder Cup record: Member of 8 European teams
(1979, 1983, 1985, 1987, 1989, 1991, 1993, 1995) Played 37,
Won 20, Lost 12, Halved 5. Captain in 1997

When Severiano Ballesteros was at the peak of his powers there was no situation too hopeless that he couldn't muster a miraculous recovery. Whether it was a low punch under a canopy of branches or a raking hook past water or sand, Seve always had the answer. He had the imagination and instinctive natural skill to recover from just about anywhere but it was never as if he had a 'laissez-faire' attitude towards the game – he cared deeply about every shot and had a steely determination to match his Spanish flair. Quite simply, Seve had the x-factor, an indescribable character trait that made him the most dashing European golfer of them all.

BELOW
Seve in action at
Wentworth in 1985.

Severiano Ballesteros was born in Santander in 1957 and grew up within close proximity of the Real Club de Golf de Pedrena. He was the youngest of four brothers all of whom became professional golfers, following in the footsteps of their uncle, Ramon Sota. One of the first Spanish players to make his mark on the world game, Ramon won a handful of professional tournaments and finished sixth in the Masters. His achievements revealed a route into lucrative tournament golf his nephew was desperate to follow.

Seve's instinctive ability to manufacture unlikely shots can be traced back to his early involvement in the game. At the age of seven he had one club – a 3-iron and would hit shots on the beach or sneak on to the course at dusk to play a few holes.

Without strategic or technical guidance he developed a unique eye for the game and learned that even a straight-faced 3-iron could be manipulated to cope with any scenario. Golf quickly became an obsession for Seve and by the age of 12 he was a scratch player. School simply didn't fit in to his masterplan and by January 1974, Ballesteros had left to become Spain's youngest professional golfer at the age of 16.

By 1976 the Spaniard was beginning to make his mark in Europe. He won his first serious event, the Dutch Open and as

leader of the Continental Order of Merit he qualified to play in the Open at Birkdale. But despite having established himself on Tour, he was still relatively unknown and the press had difficulties pronouncing his name. The 19-year-old matched Johnny Miller to share the lead after three rounds. Through the final afternoon, Seve gradually fell away as Miller accelerated but he made a late birdie rush to finish second, tied with Jack Nicklaus. The Open of 1976 offered the public a teaser of what was to come and three years later Ballesteros returned to the Lancashire coast to win his first major.

Heading into the final round at Lytham, Seve was two shots behind the reigning US Open Champion, Hale Irwin. He piled the pressure on his more experienced opponent by making a birdie two at the opening hole and by the time they reached the 3rd tee, Ballesteros was standing proud at the head of the field with a one shot lead. Typically wayward off the tee throughout the round, he constantly offered a chink of light to the chasing pack before slamming the door with an audacious recovery. At the short par-4 16th, he pushed his drive into a television compound, pitched onto the green and holed out for birdie. He took the title by three shots from Jack Nicklaus and Ben Crenshaw and at 22, was the youngest winner of the Open since Young Tom Morris.

When Ballesteros arrived at Augusta for the 1980 Masters he was a major force within the game but American audiences were yet to see

the best of him. He laid on a stunning short game display and at one stage during the final round led by a staggering 10 shots. But even at his best Seve was unpredictable and his lead was reduced to two as he stuttered through Amen Corner. He recovered well to win by four and become the first European to win the Masters.

His most memorable triumph however, came at St. Andrews in 1984. Ballesteros was up against two of the leading players of the time – Bernhard Langer and Tom Watson in a captivating three-way battle (Watson was bidding to equal Harry Vardon's record of six Open victories). Seve showed his class by parring the 17th after finding rough to the left of the fairway. Then, thinking that he needed a birdie on the last, he duly delivered. A two shot victory in spectacular style at the home of golf, confirmed Seve's place among the game's legends.

Alongside his achievements in the Majors, Seve was also a fine matchplay competitor. He played in the Ryder Cup eight times, winning 20 matches and captained the team at Valderrama in Spain in 1997. Ballesteros relished the chance to take on the best players from the States and his genuine passion for the event was crucial in raising its profile to the captivating international event that we love today.

Plagued by persistent back problems throughout his career Seve's recent attempts to compete (albeit sporadically) have proved unsuccessful. But whenever he does play, vast crowds are afforded brief glimpses of the magic that captivated audiences for over two decades. His unique, fearless eye for plotting a successful route to the hole remains one of his most attractive qualities.

ABOVE
Seve holds the Open trophy once again after winning at St. Andrews in 1984.

MIDDLE
The adoring crowd swarm around Seve, as he wins the Open at Royal Lytham, 1979.

FAR LEFT
Seve teeing off at the Belfry in the 1985 Ryder Cup.

JAMES**BRAID**

Born: Earlsferry, Fife, Scotland 1870
Died: November 27, 1950
Turned professional: 1896
Open: Winner in 1901, 1905, 1906, 1908, 1910

Born in Earlsferry in Fife in 1870, James Braid grew up between the two great golfing centres of the time, Mussleburgh and St. Andrews, and through his formative years was a regular on the links at Elie, playing and practicing whenever he could. As a teenager, Braid was a joiner by trade but worked hard to flourish on the course and by the age of 16, played to a handicap of scratch.

BELOW

Braid plays out of a bunker.

For James Braid, golf became a profession in 1893 when a friend, C R Smith offered him a job as a clubmaker for the Army and Navy store in London. Despite never having constructed a golf club before, his ability as a craftsman and knowledge of the game served him well. The Scotsman's migration south of the border also created opportunities to compete against some high-calibre opponents. In 1893 he won his first event as a professional, playing alongside his cousin, Douglas Rolland at Limpsfield. The following year he competed in a challenge match at West Drayton against J H Taylor (the reigning Open Champion), squaring the contest on the final hole. These impressive performances confirmed Braid as a player of serious note and his growing reputation allowed him to land the role as professional at Romford Golf Club in 1896 – a job that offered a secure income and an excellent platform from which to develop as a player. Then in 1904 he became the first professional at Walton Heath in Surrey.

Unlike Vardon and Taylor, James Braid had to wait for his graduation to golf's top table. He made his first appearance in the Open at St. George's in 1894 where he finished a creditable 10th and two years later at Muirfield he pocketed five pounds for finishing sixth. Then in 1897 he was runner-up to Harold Hilton at Hoylake. When his time finally arrived in 1901, he went on to win the Open five times in 10 years.

The victory in 1901 at Muirfield was emphatic. Despite shooting 80 in the final round Braid finished three shots ahead of Vardon and four in front of Taylor (the latter was bidding for his third consecutive

title). This triumph also served to redress the dramatic shift in the balance of power to English golfers at the Championship. Braid was the first Scottish winner since Willie Auchterlonie, eight years previously.

At 6ft 1ins, James Braid was a tall man with a powerful game, he had a strong grip that delivered a piercing right-to-left ball flight. At his best, his touch on the greens (which became his great weakness later in his career) complimented his powerful long game and

Braid achieved back-to-back Open wins in 1905 and 1906 at St. Andrews and Muirfield respectively. His next victory at Prestwick in 1908 was by a staggering eight shot margin over the Lancashire based golfer, Tom Ball. His fifth and final Open crown arrived at The Home of Golf in 1910 courtesy of a comfortable four shot victory over Sandy Herd. Through his decade of supremacy Braid also won the premier matchplay event that was sponsored by the News of the World on four occasions.

As the Scottish member of 'The Great Triumvirate', James Braid's astonishing list of achievements on the course provide an important chapter in the history of our game. But his lasting legacy is for being an intelligent and prolific golf course architect. His unique signature can be seen on over hundreds of courses, from Troon in Scotland to Ballybunion in Ireland. His style was to use the character of the landscape to provide natural protection and definition. Each layout is

distinctive for Braid carried no preconceptions about the type of holes he wanted to build, he simply used the natural lie of the land to determine the character of the course. The most famous of his designs include the King's and Queen's courses at Gleneagles, Rosemont and Dalmahoy. All have stood the test of time, holding firm in the face of relentless advances in equipment technology, still testing every facet of the game.

James Braid played regularly against members at Walton Heath (he is still remembered at the Surrey club with great affection) right up until his death in 1950 at the age of 80. In his latter years he would play challenge matches with the aim of beating his age and his competitive drive meant that he often succeeded.

Despite his considerable stature, James Braid was a gentle man with an instinctive game. He had a fierce determination to succeed that enabled him to catch Vardon and J H Taylor whose careers at the top level both started a step ahead. But Braid's accomplishments as a player were equalled by his considerable feats as a golf course architect. Punctuating the British landscape they provide a lasting monument to his influence on the game.

ABOVE
Braid putting on the 15th green during the Open at Troon in 1923.

FAR LEFT
Braid tees off in an exhibition match in 1926.

JOHN**DALY**

Born: Carmichael, California April 28, 1966
Turned professional: 1987
Masters: Tied 3rd in 1993
US Open: Tied 27th in 1996
Open: Winner in 1995
USPGA: Winner in 1991

When John Daly burst onto the public stage by winning the **USPGA** Championship in 1991 the golfing world suddenly had a new mega star. But Daly has always been a flawed hero, his game fluctuating between grand success and epic failure. Alcohol and marital problems have lingered throughout his career and it is precisely because he is not the perfect golfing machine that crowds find him such a captivating character.

Born in California in 1966 John Daly soon learnt not to get too attached to one particular area. His father, Jim, worked on nuclear power plants and the family moved home regularly through his early years. From the age of four, when his father handed him two shortened clubs, golf was a crucial part in John's life. Towards the end of his teenage years his interest in other sports, most notably baseball and football, waned and golf started to receive his full attention. He won important amateur championships in Arkansas and Missouri at the age of 18 and these considerable achievements landed him a place at Arkansas University. But for Daly one year in higher education was enough and in 1987, he set about plying his trade as a professional golfer.

His first three years as a tournament player were spent competing on minor tours in America and South Africa. In 1990 he finished ninth on the Hogan Tour moneylist and the self-belief gained from a consistent season provided the launch pad for a successful campaign at PGA Tour qualifying school in 1991.

Daly arrived at Crooked Stick for the USPGA Championship after an unspectacular rookie season hoping that, as ninth reserve, other players would drop out to allow him a spot in the field. Events conspired in his favour and, despite not having played the course in practice, Daly shot 69 in the opening round. He continued to attack the enormous 7,289 yard layout with typical aggression and rounds of 67, 69 and 71 followed to yield a three shot victory over Bruce Lietzke.

For many, his triumph at Crooked Stick was their first glimpse of John Daly. His

long, unrestricted swing appeared to defy the laws of physics let alone those governing a successful technique, and his exciting blend of power and aggression captivated American audiences. His first major success made him an instant celebrity but his new-found fame further unsettled his turbulent private life. Daly's fiery on-off relationship with his wife Bettye Fulford escalated into a fist-fight during a Christmas party in 1992 and he was arrested for third degree assault and suspended from the Tour. Realising that alcohol had played a destructive role in this episode he checked into an addiction treatment clinic in Arizona.

Between 1993 and 1995 Daly's private life continued to move at breakneck speed as he divorced Bettye and married Paulette Dean, who was pregnant with his child. By contrast, his on-course development stalled – his most notable achievement during this period being a third place finish in the 1993 Masters. Moving into the 1995 Open at St. Andrews there was little to suggest that Daly could win but the Old Course rewarded his aggression. Typically, JD opted for the driver as many others played for position with irons. His four round total of 282 was equalled by Constantino Rocca who

holed a remarkable 70ft putt on the final green to force a play-off. But Daly was unfazed by the Italian's dramatic finale and dominated the four additional holes, winning by four shots to pocket the £125,000 first place cheque.

John Daly's second major victory confirmed his status as one of the most naturally gifted players the game has ever seen but his addiction to alcohol remained a destructive and uncontrollable influence. In 1996 he registered just three top 10 finishes and as his game continued to fragment through the following year Paulette filed for divorce. Equipment sponsors came and went as, time after time, Daly proved himself to be a loose cannon – in the 1998 Bay Hill Invitational he recorded a score of 18 on the final hole after hitting six shots into the water.

The first signs of a revival appeared in 2001 when Daly captured the BMW International Open on the European Tour, earning a spot in the world's top 50. In 2004 he won the Buick Invitational and since then his performances have shown a level of maturity and consistency that were previously missing. Now, aged 40, Daly looks set to earn a place in the Ryder Cup for the first time in his career.

Regardless of whether he is booming 300-yard drives down the middle of the fairway or throwing his putter into a greenside lake, excitement comes guaranteed with John Daly. His two major victories were triumphs of pure natural talent, red letter days for a man plagued by personal problems. Galleries around the world continue to show their adoration for a flawed hero who at last appears to have conquered his demons.

LEFT
Daly waves to the crowd on his way to Open victory in 1995.

FAR LEFT
John Daly wins the USPGA in 1991.

LAURA**DAVIES**

Born: Coventry, England October 5, 1963
Turned professional: 1985
Kraft Nabisco Championship: 2nd in 1994
LPGA Championship: Winner in 1994, 1996
US Women's Open: Winner in 1987
Du Maurier Classic/Women's British Open:
Winner in 1996
Solheim cup record: Member of 9 European
teams (1990, 1992, 1994, 1996, 1998, 2000, 2002,
2003, 2005) Played 32, Won 16, Lost 13, Halved 3

Just as Arnold Palmer and Severiano Ballesteros had done for the men's game, so Laura Davies has shown a rare and exciting blend of power and finesse to raise the profile of women's golf. Before her arrival no British player had won major events on US soil but her instinctive game was capable of meeting the challenges of any golf course in the world. By winning national championships in a host of different countries she broke into previously unchartered territory and proved that an English girl could reach the pinnacle of professional golf.

BELOW
Davies plays in the Women's World Cup at the Gary Player Country Club, South Africa in 2006.

Laura Davies has always had a distinctive look on the course. Her sizeable frame and eye-catching dress sense suit a swing that contradicts many of the basic principles behind a successful technique. Indeed, her unique style can be traced back to her early involvement with the game.

Laura was introduced to golf by her older brother, Tony and would hitch a lift to the local golf club with her mother as she drove to work. Davies remained at the club, playing and practicing until her mother returned at the end of the day. Without any professional guidance she developed an unorthodox but instinctive technique capable of generating fast clubhead speed and impressive distance. This was coupled with a naturally deft touch that enabled her to compete throughout her teenage years with great success. Having made an impact with the Surrey county girls team, she went on to win both South East and Intermediate English Championships before playing in the 1984 Curtis Cup.

Her ascent through the amateur ranks had successfully prepared Davies for life on Tour by 1985. But to finance her travels around Europe, she was forced to borrow £1,000 from her mother. The pressure of this financial burden and the desperate desire to prove herself at the top level inspired Davies to a second place finish at the Hennessy Cognac Ladies Cup in Paris just two weeks after setting out on Tour. A cheque for £4,000 allowed Davies to repay

her mother's generosity and continue her successful rookie season – she finished 11th in the US Women's Open before winning the same title in Britain.

When she arrived at Plainfield in New Jersey for the US Women's Open of 1987 she was still relatively unknown. But after 72 holes Davies had announced herself to the world, tying JoAnne Carter and Ayako Okamoto for the lead. No British player had ever won the event and up against far more experienced opponents, few expected Davies to prevail in the 18-hole play-off that ensued. But her powerful game intensified the pressure on her opponents and she won with a score of 71. This exciting victory marked a seminal moment in the evolution of the LPGA Tour. Davies had qualified to play in the event through her performances in Europe and was not a member of the US Tour. The LPGA were forced to amend their constitution to grant the winner of the Open automatic membership to the Tour.

Despite her inception to the most lucrative of female Tours in 1987, Davies retained her ambition to compete on different stages around the world throughout her career. In 1988 she finished 15th on the LPGA Tour moneylist and second in Europe as well as winning once in Japan. She always relished the challenge of pitting her wits against a variety of different courses and fields and in 1994 she became the first player to win on five different Tours in the same year. At this time she was the world's number one player and by taking her dynamic game to all corners of the globe was satisfying her responsibility as the most important ambassador for the sport.

Laura Davies reached the peak of her powers between 1994 and 1996. She won 23 times around the world during this period including three major championships. Her fierce battle at the top

of the world rankings with Annika Sorenstam captivated audiences and proved that women's golf was capable of producing genuine sporting superstars.

In addition to helping the spread of women's golf, Laura Davies was also an important figure in the growth of the Solheim Cup. The event was first played in 1990 at Lake Nona in Florida and Davies was part of a European team that were soundly thrashed by their American rivals. At this time many feared the gulf between the two sides would render future encounters pointless but in 1992, Europe won at Dalmahoy and Davies collected three points from three matches. Now into her 40s, she remains an ever-present and her talismanic performances have been essential to the continued competitiveness of the Solheim Cup.

Like many of the great golfers featured in this book, Davies has enjoyed a long career at the highest level and it certainly isn't over yet. Not only is she a regular winner but she plays with a dynamic, all-or-nothing style that embraces power and delicacy in equal measures. She paved the way for fellow Europeans to embark on successful international careers and raised the quality of competition for appreciative audiences all around the world.

ABOVE
Davies in Solheim Cup action in 2005.

FAR LEFT
Laura Davies poses with the Solheim Cup in 2002.

ERNIE
ELS

Born: Johannesburg, South Africa October 17, 1969
Turned professional: 1989
Masters: 2nd in 2000 and 2004
US Open: Winner in 1994, 1997
Open: Winner in 2002
USPGA: Tied 3rd in 1995

Watching Ernie Els boom 300-yard drives and produce delicate chips shots without breaking a sweat makes our notoriously taxing game appear simple. The 6ft 3ins South African swings with an elegance and poise that defies his physical make-up and his effortless power has earned him the nickname, "The Big Easy" . Like the great South African players before him, Ernie Els has been a treasured ambassador for the sport, raising the popularity and profile of the game by competing in all corners of the globe. Despite the supremacy of Tiger Woods, Ernie Els has emerged as a world class performer with three majors and a host of Tour titles to his name.

BELOW
Els plays out of a bunker in the 2005 Asian Open.

Throughout his early years, Ernie Els was a keen and talented sportsman playing cricket, tennis and rugby as well as golf. In fact it was only when he reached the age of 14, that Els picked golf over tennis – he was Eastern Transvaal Junior tennis Champion at 13. With his attention undivided he soon collected important junior titles. In 1984 he travelled to San Diego to compete in the boys category (ages 13 to 14) of the Junior World Championship and emerged victorious from a field that included Phil Mickleson. Two years later he won the South African Amateur and this triggered a flood of offers from American Universities but Els chose to complete his education in South Africa and when he reached the age of 19, turned professional in 1989.

Competing on the Southern Africa Tour (now known as the Sunshine Tour), Els made his mark in 1992. In one season he accumulated six victories including the three major South African events – the Open, PGA and Masters. By equalling Gary Player's achievement his early promise was confirmed and Els was ready to tackle the best players in the world.

In 1993 he announced himself to the world by becoming the first player to complete all four British Open rounds in the 60s. This was an astonishing feat on one of the most fearsome tracks on the Open rota, St. George's but it was only good enough for sixth place. This performance

provided a teaser for what would unfold the following year at the US Open.

In 1994 the Championship was making its seventh appearance at Oakmont and with a list of previous winners that includes Nicklaus, Hogan and Miller the USGA were confident that the very best would rise to the top. After four rounds Els was locked at the head of the leaderboard alongside Loren Roberts and Colin Montgomerie. An 18-hole three-way play-off eliminated the Scot but was unable to separate the other two. Els outlasted his American opponent finally prevailing on the 20th hole to become a major winner for the first time, aged 24.

As US Open Champion, Els was still developing his game and the confidence gained from winning his first major was the launchpad for further success in the 90s. In 1997 he completed a hat-trick of World Matchplay titles and the following year he claimed his second US Open crown. Els overtook Tom Lehman with a final round 69 and once again narrowly held off the challenge of Colin Montgomerie. His victory at Congressional was worth far more than the half a million dollar prizefund – it confirmed the South African as the official world number one.

Although he continued to win regularly on various Tours around the world, Ernie Els remained winless in the big four until 2002. This barren spell can be explained in part by the rise to prominence of Tiger

Woods. In 2000 the American was in his prime, winning three consecutive majors pushing Els down into second place twice. That year 'The Big Easy' also finished second in the Masters behind Vijay Singh and the disappointment of three near misses hit hard – Els remained winless on the PGA Tour the following year.

Ernie Els hit back in 2002 winning six times worldwide including the Open at Muirfield. With nine holes left to play he held a commanding three-stroke lead and appeared in total command of his game. But the Claret Jug was the one trophy he yearned for more than any other and in his desperation to finish the job, nerves had a detrimental affect on his golf. His commanding lead evaporated leaving him in a four way play-off with Thomas Levet, Stuart Appleby and Steve Elkington. Despite his disappointing finale, Els knew that he was the form runner and made five consecutive pars under intense pressure to earn his third major title the hard way.

Since winning the Open of 2002, Ernie Els has captured his first World Golf Championship and his sixth World Matchplay. He has also finished at the top of the European Tour's order of merit twice. Now aged 36, his immense power and deft touch are allied by a wealth of experience that continues to make him one of the world's most dangerous competitors.

ABOVE
Els in the final round of the Open in 2002, which he went on to win.

FAR LEFT
Ernie Els with the US Open trophy in 1997.

NICK
FALDO

Born: Welwyn Garden City, England July 18, 1957
Turned professional: 1976
Masters: Winner in 1989, 1990, 1996
US Open: 2nd in 1988
Open: Winner in 1987, 1990, 1992
USPGA: Tied 2nd in 1992
Ryder Cup record: Member of 11 European teams (1977, 1979, 1981, 1983, 1985, 1987, 1989, 1991, 1993, 1995, 1997). Played 46, Won 23, Lost 19, Halved 4

Two of the game's most exciting commodities, Jack Nicklaus and Augusta National, combined to ignite Nick Faldo's passion for golf in 1971. Aged 13 he watched the Masters unfold on his parents' brand new colour television set and, despite never having played golf before, was suddenly hooked. Faldo showed maturity beyond his years by taking lessons with Ian Connelly, the professional at Welwyn Garden City, and practicing tirelessly for months before actually venturing onto the golf course. Without concerning himself with scores or competing under pressure Faldo grooved the fundamental swing mechanics so crucial for a man of his height and build. This hard work soon paid off and within two years Faldo was playing off a handicap of plus one.

During his amateur career Faldo represented England at various levels but his greatest achievement was to win the English Amateur Championship in 1975, aged 18. With this triumph at the top of his CV he turned professional the following year.

A creditable 58th position in his first European Tour Order of Merit was followed by a more consistent 1977 season. That year he finished eighth on the moneylist, playing his way into the Ryder Cup at Royal Lytham.

As a Ryder Cup rookie his mental strength soon became evident as he forged an unbeaten partnership with fellow Englishman Peter Oosterhuis, before beating the reigning Masters and Open champion, Tom Watson, in the final day singles. The European team was soundly beaten but Faldo had announced himself on the world stage.

From here Faldo made a relentless ascent through the world rankings and won the European Tour Order of Merit in 1983. By the end of the following year Faldo had 11 European Tour titles and four Ryder Cup appearances to his name. But Faldo was yet to succeed at the very highest level a fact that really hit home when he was forced to watch two of his greatest

rivals, Sandy Lyle and Seve Ballesteros, picking up major honours.

Enter David Leadbetter, a young Zimbabwian-born golf coach who was beginning to make his name on tour. Leadbetter told Faldo that to win a major he would need a technique strong enough to withstand the most intense pressure. For all of its aesthetic beauty, Leadbetter felt that Faldo's swing was cursed by too many moving parts that when placed under the microscope could throw the whole swing out of kilter. Together, Faldo and Leadbetter spent two years rebuilding his swing, during which time he continued to compete but the calibre of his performances dropped drastically. By the end of 1986 he had lost his US Tour card and many questioned if the Englishman was a spent force.

These questions were answered emphatically in 1987.

That year the Open took place at Muirfield, one of the most demanding layouts on the tournament rota. When the wind blew during the final afternoon it became a battle of attrition but Faldo made 18 consecutive pars to record a final round 71. A faultless display of clean ball striking and nerveless short game skill reeled in Paul Azinger, who had led going into the last day.

If ever Faldo needed an endorsement of the previous two years hard work, it arrived emphatically that day in July.

From this success came the self-belief that his swing would thrive under pressure and his results continued to improve. He finished second eight times in 1988, including after a play-off with Curtis Strange for the US Open.

Despite tasting defeat, this head-to-head experience proved invaluable as Faldo defeated another American, Scott Hoch in a play-off for the 1989 Masters. There followed another Green Jacket and a second Open title in 1990 and during this period Faldo was comfortably the world's best player.

Each of the Englishman's major triumphs are memorable for their sheer tenacity but perhaps his most dramatic success came as he won his final Masters in 1996. Greg Norman had been in imperious form and held a six-shot lead going into the final round but the golfing world watched through their fingers as the Australian's confidence shattered and his long game imploded. Given a glimpse of his playing partner's fragility, Faldo typically raised his game and after a final round 67, compared to Norman's 78, won by five shots.

Having been married three times it would be fair to assume that Nick Faldo's relentless pursuit of glory has had a detrimental impact on his private life. But despite lingering turmoil off the course, his determination and focus on it has never wavered. From the very start, his story is one of hard graft and a stern will to succeed, traits that were the hallmarks of his greatest triumphs.

FAR LEFT
Nick Faldo with the Claret Jug in 1987.

MIDDLE
Watched by Fanny Sunesson his caddie for many years, Faldo plays out of a bunker on his way to a third Masters.

BELOW
Nick Faldo receives his Green Jacket in 1996.

WALTER
HAGEN

Born: Rochester, New York December 21, 1892

Died: October 5, 1969

Turned professional: 1901

US Open: Winner in 1914, 1919

Open: Winner in 1922, 1924, 1928, 1929

USPGA: Winner in 1921, 1924, 1925, 1926, 1927

Ryder Cup record: Captained 6 US teams, playing in 5 of those matches (1927, 1929, 1931, 1933, 1935 (1937)). Played 9, Won 7, Lost 1, Halved 1

Golf and fashion have always been uneasy bedfellows. Without team uniforms or the demands of strenuous exercise dictating basic restrictions, golfers have been free to express their personalities through their clothing. But until Walter Hagen arrived in the early 1900s, players tended to be suited and booted in much the same way with a smart, sophisticated look golfers had always dressed conservatively. Hagen was the first man to really stretch these boundaries and with his natural charm coupled with an immense talent on the course he broadened the appeal of the game.

Walter Hagen hailed from a blue collar, working class family from Rochester in New York. Living within easy reach of the local country club, he worked his way up from caddie to club maker to head professional by the age of 19. Through these impressionable years, he was in regular contact with wealthy club members, their lavish lifestyles and elegant attire left an indelible mark on the young man.

His early graduation to head professional paid well – $1200 for eight months of the year as well as $2 per lesson – so during the four winter months, he was free to enter professional events and it was as a player that Hagen found the spotlight he adored. Having performed well in the US Open of 1913 (he finished in a tie for fourth), he started to develop a reputation as a dangerous competitor. In 1914 a member of his Rochester club offered to pay his travel expenses so that he could return to the US Open in Chicago. Hagen rewarded his sponsor's faith by shooting a record low 68 in the opening round. He led the event from start to finish to claim his first major title.

BELOW
Hagen plays a shot in front of a small crowd in 1920.

This victory opened the world to Hagen – he was now a man in demand. During the war he travelled across America playing challenge matches and charity events and endorsing products. His relaxed, lively character was attractive to sponsors as in a world torn apart by bloody conflict, he was able to appreciate that golf was essentially a showbusiness.

In 1919 Hagen took a job as head professional at Oakland Hills. Situated in affluent Detroit, it appeared to be the ideal position, offering a comfortable and secure living. But after winning the US Open for the second time that year, Hagen realised that he could make good money as a player without having the restrictive responsibilities of a club pro. He promptly left his post at Oakland Hills to become the first solely playing professional.

When the war in Europe finished, Hagen was ready to expand his horizons and he crossed the Atlantic for the first time on the Maureitania in 1920, as the reigning US Open Champion. The British public were keen to see just how good the best from the US would be and his presence at Royal Cinque Ports created an unprecedented level of interest.

By this time Hagen had the means to live the lavish lifestyle he craved and he arrived at Deal on the Kent coast, chauffeur driven in a hired Daimler. The rules of the club dictated that players should not enter the clubhouse to change their shoes so Hagen chose to do so in his car which was parked directly outside the front of the clubhouse!

The Little Book of **GOLF** LEGENDS

Emerging from his ostentatious changing room, Hagen cut a striking figure in black and white, dressed from head to toe in the finest materials. Unfortunately, his golf failed to live up to his snappy outfits and he finished 53rd in a field of 54.

Despite this disappointing display, Hagen showed his devotion to the event for many years to come and in 1922 he took the title. In 1924, after arriving late for qualifying and persuading the organisers to let him compete, he won again. This victory marked a seminal moment in the evolution of our treasured Championship.

Until this point, the Open field was dominated by British players. After Hagen's victory in 1924 the top Americans recognised the importance of the Championship and regularly travelled to Britain, strengthening the competition. Thanks to Hagen's influence, the tournament that we hold in such high regard today became truly international.

Walter Hagen's record in the two major Opens drifts into obscurity when compared to his performances in the USPGA. Until 1958, the USPGA was the premier matchplay event in the tournament calendar and Hagen entered six times from 1924 and only lost once in 30 matches.

Walter Hagen's reputation remains as a showman both on and off the course, he was a notorious ladies man who was married twice and loved a party. He became a true golfing superstar, bringing life and colour to an intrinsically conservative game. Furthermore, he paved the way for the likes of Jimmy Demaret, Payne Stewart and Ian Poulter to express their characters through their eye-catching clothing.

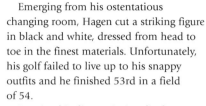

BEN
HOGAN

Born: Dublin, Texas August 13, 1912
Died: July 25, 1997
Masters: Winner in 1951, 1953,
US Open: Winner in 1948, 1950, 1951, 1953
Open: Winner in 1953
USPGA: Winner in 1946, 1948
Ryder Cup record: Member of 2 US teams (1947, 1951). Played 3, Won 3. Captain in 1947, 1949, 1967

More than any other player featured in this book, Ben Hogan fought adversity to forge a successful career in golf. The tragedy of his father's suicide, the desperate struggle to make ends meet and the car crash that nearly killed him all contributed to the steely character of one of the finest golfers in the history of the sport. At his best Hogan had an unerring accuracy and deadly short-range putting stroke to ally his single-minded determination.

BELOW
Hogan plays a short shot as the gallery looks on, 1940.

Ben Hogan was born in Dublin, Texas, in 1912. His father was a mechanic by trade but as the Depression hit in the 1920s he found work hard to come by and struggled to earn enough money to support his family. In the face of mounting financial pressure and persistent health worries Hogan's father shot himself – Ben was just nine years old at the time.

Not that he needed to be told but this tragedy underlined the importance of earning a secure living and Hogan's involvement in golf started as a boy, earning cash by caddying for members at the local Glen Garden Club. He would play whenever the opportunity arose and during his teens entered amateur state events whenever possible. Success may have been limited but Hogan's knowledge of the game was improving all the time and he turned professional at the age of 19.

For the next nine years Hogan would pursue his dream of making it on Tour without any notable success. In 1937 he married Valerie Fox and the two travelled the country in the desperate hope that Ben would make a substantial cheque to cover their expenses. The breakthrough finally came in 1940 when the 28-year-old Hogan took the North and South Open at Pinehurst. The confidence gained from this overdue victory enabled him to sustain a higher level of performance and he captured the US Tour moneylist in 1940, 41 and 42. But World War II struck just as his career was gathering momentum and Hogan joined

The Little Book of **GOLF** LEGENDS

the US Army Air Corps where he served for three years. On his return to competition in 1946 Hogan, or "The Hawk" as he had become known, won his first major – the USPGA. This victory was made even sweeter having narrowly missed out in both the Masters and US Open earlier that year.

Despite stepping up to the highest level of international golf Hogan realised that to fulfill his potential he had to rid himself of the destructive hook that remained a part of his armoury. In 1947, he practiced hard to turn his natural ball flight from a draw into a fade. The result was a shorter but far more consistent shot that he could rely on under pressure. These changes made him a more potent force and in 1948 he won the US Open and USPGA.

By the start of 1949 Hogan's career was in full swing and he was a serious threat whenever he teed up. But on February 2nd, Hogan was involved in a horrific car crash that left him with numerous broken bones. He spent two months in hospital and did not play golf for the best part of a year.

Walking with a limp Hogan returned to competitive action at the 1950 US Open knowing that 36 holes on the final day might be too much for his weakened frame. But with typical

tenacity he applied himself to the task at hand and managed to force a play-off with George Fazio and Lloyd Mancrum. This meant another round the following day but Hogan mustered the strength for an incredible 69 to take the title. This courageous victory made Ben Hogan the darling of the American public.

Hogan had previously travelled to Britain at the end of 1949 as the non-playing captain of the American Ryder Cup side. It would be fair to say that despite winning the match he did not enjoy the experience and by 1953 was yet to enter the Open. But after winning the US Open and Masters that year, he realised that to be remembered as a great champion he needed to complete the British leg of the Grand Slam. He arrived in Scotland to face a brutal 7,200 yard test on a windswept Carnoustie. Showing supreme ball control in difficult conditions, he won by four shots from a group of players that included Peter Thompson.

Hogan was unable to make it back to the States in time for the USPGA but it didn't matter. Aged 40, he had completed the Grand Slam and on his return to New York was given a hero's welcome. His triumph at Carnoustie capped a remarkable year but his major triumphs of 1953 were his last. The yips plagued him for the rest of his career but having triumphed over adversity Hogan had nothing left to prove.

FAR LEFT
Hogan on the practice ground.

MIDDLE
Hogan reminds everyone that he has won the Chicago Open in 1941.

BELOW
Ben Hogan wins the Open in 1953.

BOBBY**JONES**

Born: Atlanta, Georgia March 17, 1902
Died: December 18, 1971
US Open: Winner in 1923, 1926, 1929, 1930
Open: Winner in 1926, 1927, 1930

When Bobby Jones won the **US Amateur Championship of 1930** he became the only golfer in history to capture the national and amateur titles of Britain and America in the same year. "The Impregnable Quadrilateral" as it became known, is a unique achievement that will almost certainly remain untouched. His victories of 1930 were the glorious finale to a seven year period of supremacy in which Jones won seven Opens and six Amateur Championships. But the strain of travelling the world to compete in front of vast, expectant galleries and the stress of living up to his own high expectations pushed him into retirement at the tender age of 28. Thus, memories of **Bobby Jones** the golfer are of a stylish man in his peak with a smooth swing and a devastating ability to win.

BELOW
Jones tees off, 1921.

As a child, Bobby Jones suffered perpetual digestive problems and was unable to take solid foods. His ailment forced his parents to move from Atlanta city to the suburbs in the hope that cleaner air would help their son's health. Their new home was within close proximity of the golf club at East Lake and aged five Jones's health steadily improved as he started to play. Like many golfers who begin at an early age, Jones copied the technique of a respected player. Stewart Maiden was the professional at East Lake and without any specific guidance, Jones simply mimicked his swing.

By the age of 13, he had won both junior and senior East Lake club championships and the following year he made his debut in the US Amateur at Merion Cricket Club. The teenager attracted serious media interest as he progressed to the third round of the matchplay phase where he was knocked out by defending champion, Bob Gardner.

Few doubted that Jones was a champion of the future but he was a temperamental young man, prone to throwing clubs and losing his head at the crucial moment. Over the next seven years he would continue to compete in major events without success. In 1921, Jones travelled to

Britain to compete in the inaugural Walker Cup matches at Hoylake and after a victorious campaign, he entered the Open at St. Andrews. But after 10 disastrous holes of his third round, he stormed off the course. The 19-year-old was castigated by the press and it was apparent for all to see that his immaturity was costing him dear.

By 1923 Jones had learned to temper his youthful impetuosity and his breakthrough duly arrived at the US Open at Inwood, New York. He had one hand on the trophy with three holes of his final round left to play but finished with two bogeys and a double bogey to fall back into a tie with Bobby Cruickshank. Questions over his mental strength however, were quashed as Jones struck a perfect 4-iron approach to the final green to close out the head-to-head battle with a score of 76 to Cruickshank's 78.

This initial success triggered an avalanche of titles and records over the next seven years. Through this period he won 13 major events and was always either US Open or Amateur champion. He won the British Open three times, his first in 1926 pitted him against Al Waltrous in an exciting final round dual over the links at Hoylake. At the 17th Jones pulled his tee shot into a sandy waste area to the left of the fairway. Faced with 175 yards to the flag, he fired a fearless long iron approach into the heart of the green.

Unnerved by his opponent's miraculous recovery, Waltrous three putted. When Jones went on to win the US Open that year, he became the first player to capture the two major national championships in the same season.

As Bobby Jones reached his mid-20s, he had just one important title left to win – the British Amateur. The victory he craved arrived in 1930 at St. Andrews. Such was his popularity among the British public, that it is estimated between 12 and 15,000 spectators travelled to watch his fourth round match against Cyril Tolley. Jones won an epic encounter on the 19th hole and progressed through five more matches in three days to take the title. He added the Open at Hoylake and US Open at Interlachen to his season's successes before arriving back at Merion for the US Amateur. Victory at the venue of his first ever major appearance would guarantee Jones golfing immortality and he marched mercilessly to the title winning each of his five matches by no worse than 5 and 4.

While the record books show a man at the top of his profession, dominating fields with apparent ease, the reality was somewhat less glorious. His great friend and journalist OB Keeler always described how Jones suffered terribly with stress during each event. He cared desperately about performing to his absolute optimum and the strain of competing successfully at the highest level for over a decade had taken its toll. In November 1930, Jones announced his retirement.

At the age of 28, Bobby Jones felt that he had achieved all he could as an amateur golfer and embarked on a law career in Atlanta. But there was to be one last chapter in his involvement with the game. Under his supervision, Augusta National was designed by Alister Mackenzie and opened in 1933. The following year the US Masters was born as Jones realised his ambition to establish an invitational strokeplay event between the best players in the world.

BOBBY**LOCKE**

Born: Germiston, South Africa November 20, 1917
Turned professional: 1938
Masters: Tied for 13th in 1949
US Open: 3rd in 1947 and 1951
Open: Winner in 1949, 1950, 1952, 1957

The first of the great South African golfers, Bobby Locke travelled the world to reach the very top of his profession. Winning important tournaments on three separate continents, his most notable achievement was to triumph in our Open Championship on four occasions. A big man with a rounded swing, Locke hit the ball with a raking draw that verged on a hook and had one of the deadliest putting strokes the game has ever seen. He would navigate his way around the course at his own sedate pace and his unique style, chirpy character and natural talent made him stand out whenever he played.

Born Arthur D'Arcy Locke in 1917 he quickly became known as Bobby for his love of the great Bobby Jones. Locke's amateur career was brief by comparison to the great American's but provided a glimpse of the glory that was to follow. His first notable triumph came in 1931, at the age of 14, when he won the South African Boys Championship. Then three years later he made his mark on the men's amateur scene by winning the South African Open and Amateur Championships. When he repeated this double in 1937 it confirmed his status as one of the leading amateurs in the game and the following year he graduated to the paid ranks.

As a professional, Locke was quick to announce himself on the world stage, winning the Irish, New Zealand and South African Opens in 1938. But just as his career was blossoming World War II started and Locke joined the South African air force as a bomber pilot, carrying out tours of duty in the western desert and the Mediterranean. On his return to competition in 1946 his two and a half year hiatus from the game did not appear to have hampered his progress as a player as, despite being a few pounds heavier, he won twice in Britain and claimed another South African Open title.

Following the advice of Walter Hagen, Locke then travelled to America in 1947 to become a full time tournament

professional. The move brought immediate success as he won four of the first six events that he played in. For three years Locke was a regular on the American circuit, taking at least one title per season and, despite never actually winning, he finished third twice and fourth twice in the US Open. But the story of Bobby Locke's time in the States is not quite as glorious as the records suggest. He was a prolific foreign winner with a deliberate style on the course that made him unpopular with the American crowds (he was often accused of slow play). And when he crossed the Atlantic to compete in Britain in 1949, he was deemed to have broken important contracts and the USGA tried to ban him from entering American tournaments.

This incident encouraged Locke to shift his attention to Europe and in 1949 he won the first of his four Open titles at Sandwich in Kent. After tying with Harry Bradshaw on a four round total of 283, Locke thrashed his accomplished opponent by 12 strokes over a 36-hole play-off.

The following year, he defended his crown on the west coast of Scotland at Royal Troon, beating Roberto DiVicenzo by two shots. Then in 1952 he defeated his arch rival Peter Thompson by one stroke at Royal Lytham & St. Annes in Lancashire.

However, Locke's final major triumph at St. Andrews in 1957 was marred by controversy. On the 18th green of the final round, Locke moved his marker by the length of his putterhead to clear a route to the hole for his playing partner

Bruce Crampton. Locke forgot to return the marker to its original spot and putted out to complete a three-shot victory over Peter Thompson. The incident was later reported to rules officials at the R&A but it was decided that Locke had not received any advantage by moving his ball and was not disqualified. This unfortunate episode understandably rocked the South African so by way of a strange self-punishment he vowed never to play in plus fours again!

During the 50s the intense rivalry between Locke and his Australian counterpart Peter Thompson lit up the game and the pair won eight Open titles in 10 years. But Locke's victory in 1957 was his last great triumph as three years later he was involved in a horrific car crash that left him in a coma for several days. He was incredibly fortunate to survive the accident but the permanent damage to his left eye hampered his future performances on the golf course.

His colourful career slowly tailed off but Locke had already reached the pinnacle of his profession, revealing a route to success for the great South African players that followed. His quirky but laid-back character and distinctive style are still fondly remembered, especially in Britain.

ABOVE
Locke plays out of a bunker at the 1953 Open, Carnoustie.

FAR LEFT
Bobby Locke with the Open trophy.

SANDY**LYLE**

Born: Shrewsbury, England February 9, 1958
Turned professional: 1977
Masters: Winner in 1988
US Open: Tied 16th in 1991
Open: Winner in 1985
USPGA: Tied 16th in 1991
Ryder Cup record: Member of 5 European
teams (1979, 981, 1983, 1985, 1987). Played 18,
Won 7, Lost 9, Halved 2

In his prime, Sandy Lyle was undoubtedly one of the greatest strikers of a golf ball the sport has ever seen. It is therefore rather fitting that the Scot who was born in England will forever be remembered for a perfectly struck 7-iron that crowned him the first British winner of the US Masters.

Lyle had led the 1988 Masters from the first round and at the start of the final day held a two shot lead over Mark Calcavecchia and Ben Crenshaw. But three putts on the treacherous 11th green were followed by a double bogey at 12, where his tee shot found water. Amen Corner looked to have taken another victim as Lyle now trailed Calcavecchia. But the Scot's challenge regained momentum as he made a crucial birdie on the 16th and he reached the final tee needing a par to force a play-off with his American rival.

Having found sand to the left of the 18th fairway with his usually reliable 1-iron, Lyle was faced with 145 yards uphill to a notoriously dangerous green. This was an all-or-nothing moment, a defining passage of play that required total commitment to a technically sound swing. The result was a crisp 7-iron approach that finished around 12ft from the flag, a shot that is now treasured as a glorious part of Augustan folklore. He rolled home the putt and the green jacket was in Scottish hands.

From 1955, Sandy's Glaswegian father, Alex was the head professional at Hawkstone Park and it was in Shropshire that Sandy was born in 1958. Despite growing up around the game, his decision to pursue it seriously came as he watched Tony Jacklin win the 1969 Open at Royal Lytham. Aged 11, Lyle was driven to emulate his hero's spectacular achievement and soon excelled as a talented junior, regularly competing in mens competitions. By the age of 15 his handicap was down to scratch and he was forging an impressive amateur career. When the inevitable opportunity to step up from county to international level arrived in the early 70s,

Sandy and Alex had a difficult decision to make. Travelling to and from Scotland would have been both costly and time consuming, so the Lyle's decided that Sandy should represent England.

In 1975, at the age of 17, he won international caps at boys, youths and senior levels, he also won the English Open Amateur beating Nick Faldo in the process. Two years later, after representing GB&I in the Walker Cup he turned professional, regaining his identity as a true Scot.

For many, life in the professional ranks comes as a shock that requires years of gradual adjustment, but for Lyle the switch brought instant success as he won the qualifying school for the European Tour then immediately tasted victory at the Nigerian Open. In his first season in the paid ranks he finished 49th on the European Tour Order of Merit, winning the Henry Cotton prize for Rookie of the Year.

During the next decade, Lyle emerged as one of the best players in the world. His consistently high calibre performances, brought a steady flow of titles including the European Open in 1979, the individual World Cup in 1980 (representing Scotland) and the Italian Open in 1984.

By 1985, Lyle seemed destined to claim one of the game's most prestigious prizes for himself. But one month prior to the Open at St. George's, the Scot was hopelessly out of touch. Competing in the Irish Open at Royal Dublin, he needed a par four on the final hole of his opening round to break 90. When he hit his second shot out of bounds, he decided not to return a score. Failure in Ireland inspired Lyle to spend crucial time working on his swing under the tutelage his father and by mid-July his game was back in shape.

Going into the final round at Royal St. George's, Lyle was sitting three shots behind Bernhard Langer and David Graham. A steady front

nine kept him in touch with the leaders and when he made back-to-back birdies at 14 and 15, victory became a real possibility. However, the 468-yard par-4 18th at Sandwich is one of the most demanding finishing holes on the Open rota and when Lyle pulled his second left of the green a poor chip was followed by two putts and a play-off seemed likely. But the other players failed to capitalise on Lyle's mistake and he became the first British winner of the Open since his hero, Tony Jacklin, 16 years earlier.

The confidence gained from this triumph was the springboard for success in America – he won the Greater Greensboro Open in 1986 and the flagship Tournament Players Championship in 1987. Victory at Augusta in 1988 proved that Lyle had a truly global game that was fit for any course in the world. That year he also won the World Matchplay Championship at Wentworth proving he was also a master of the head-to-head format.

For 30-year-old Sandy Lyle, 1988 was the annus mirabilis that he was never able to recreate. His performances slowly tailed off and top finishes became more and more infrequent. His final European Tour victory came as early as 1992 at the Volvo Masters in Valderamma.

In the years following 1988, Lyle stepped aside to let the likes of Nick Faldo and Seve Ballesteros grab the limelight but the nature of his two major victories still evoke fond memories from those who were desperate to see a breakthrough British success. Furthermore, his triumphs placed European golfers firmly on the international map.

FAR LEFT
Sandy Lyle poses with his family in 1985, after winning the Open.

MIDDLE
Lyle plays out of a bunker at Augusta on his way to winning the Masters.

BELOW
Sandy Lyle receives his Green Jacket from Larry Mize in 1988.

COLIN
MONTGOMERIE

Born: Glasgow, Scotland July 23, 1963
Turned professional: 1987
Masters: Tied 8th in 1998
US Open: 2nd in 1997, tied 2nd in 2006
Open: 2nd in 2005
USPGA: 2nd in 1995
Ryder Cup record: Member of 8 European teams (1991, 1993, 1995, 1997, 1999, 2002, 2004, 2006) Played 36, Won 20, Lost 9, Halved 7

If performances in the four biggest tournaments were the only true measure of a player's greatness then Colin Montgomerie would not have earned his place in this book of golfing legends. But outside the toughest strokeplay events is a tournament schedule that runs throughout the year, posing unique challenges on a variety of different courses. Competing regularly on Tour requires a level of consistency that success in the majors simply does not, and Colin Montgomerie proved his class by becoming the most prolific money winner in European Tour history. Furthermore, his talismanic performances in six Ryder Cups have been the single most important factor in the increased potency of the European team.

BELOW
Montgomerie plays in the 2005 Hong Kong Open.

Born in Glasgow in 1963, Colin Montgomerie is the son of a former secretary at Royal Troon. Growing up on this windy linksland it was inevitable that he and his brother Douglas would develop a healthy passion for the game. Montgomerie was afforded the time to pursue his interest in golf and compete regularly while at Strathallan public school. Having then won a scholarship to Houston Baptist University in Texas his amateur career progressed at a fair pace. He won the 1983 Scottish Youths title and played twice in the Walker Cup before winning the Scottish Amateur Championship in 1987. But despite these considerable achievements it was never Monty's goal to become a professional golfer. Instead, he wanted to use his degree in business management and law to forge a career in golf away from the course. But after graduating from university Montgomerie decided to give life on Tour a try and he turned pro in 1987.

In his first season on the European Tour, Monty revealed his aptitude for team golf, playing for Scotland in the Alfred Dunhill Cup and World Cup. It was an impressive debut season in which he amassed almost £40,000 to become the European Tour's rookie of the year. His maiden victory arrived the following season at the Portuguese Open.

Throughout the 90s Monty was a prolific winner on the European Tour. His unerring accuracy off the tee and precise distance control enabled him to compete on any golf course on the continent. He won tournaments in Sweden, Holland, France and Spain as well as in Britain and captured an astonishing seven consecutive Order of Merit titles. Returning year after year with the determination to maintain his stranglehold over European fields, Montgomerie became the most successful player in the history of the European Tour.

And yet despite consistently proving that he is a world class performer Montgomerie has never been able to make his mark in the majors. With its demands on accuracy and crisp ball striking the Scot has always had the right game for the US Open. At Oakmont in 1994 Montgomerie found himself in a play-off with Ernie Els and Loren Roberts but a round of 78 left him four shots adrift and he was forced to settle back into a tie for second. He also finished second in 1997, just one shot behind the same South African winner. At the 1995 USPGA Steve Elkington sunk a 25ft putt on the first play-off hole to crush his hopes again. It would appear that the burden carried by the memory of these near misses, coupled with the pressure of meeting his major expectations, has made capturing one of the big four a hurdle the Scotsman simply cannot jump.

Colin Montgomerie's failure to capture any of the big four is a glaring omission on his vast list of

achievements, especially when you consider his record in the Ryder Cup. The Scot has played every year since 1991, never losing a singles match and his career total of 21½ points makes him one of the most successful Ryder Cup players of all time. His most impressive performance was at Oakland Hills in 2004 when after a turbulent year off the course, in which he divorced his wife Eimear, Monty had failed to qualify outright for the team and required a captain's pick from Bernhard Langer. The 41-year-old Scot repaid his friend's faith by prevailing in three of his four matches and it was fitting that Montgomerie should sink the winning putt as Europe romped to an 18½ to 9½ victory.

His role in the triumph at Oakland Hills was the springboard for even greater success in 2005. A second place finish in the Open and victory at the Dunhill Cup (both at the home of golf) returned Montgomerie to the top of the European Tour Order of Merit. That he should scale these heights at the age of 42, having already achieved this milestone seven times previously, is a testament to his determination. But despite his regular victories on Tour and his heroic performances in the Ryder Cup, Montgomerie will not rest easy until he fulfills his potential by winning one of the four biggest prizes.

ABOVE

Montgomerie on the sixth tee at St. Andrews, 2005.

FAR LEFT

Colin Montgomerie celebrates victory over the USA in the Ryder Cup, 2004.

OLDTOM
MORRIS

Born: St. Andrews, Scotland June 16, 1821
Died: May 24, 1908
Turned professional: 1851
Open: Winner in 1861, 1862, 1864, 1867

In an age when a player's true class is measured by the number of majors he wins and the money he pockets through a seasonal schedule that spans the breadth of the globe, it is hard to quantify the achievements of Old Tom Morris. When he was born in 1821 golf was very much a pastime for the privileged minority, with no professionals or major tournaments. Morris was the first man to make a living as a club pro and he was a regular competitor in the embryonic stages of the Open Championship. Today he is fondly remembered as the founding father of professional golfers.

Old Tom's initial association with the game can be traced back to his job as apprentice to the St. Andrews club, and ball maker Alan Robertson. A skilled craftsman, Robertson was also one of the most accomplished players of the time – in 1858 he became the first man to break 80 at St. Andrews, a record that stood for 30 years. Through the influence of Robertson, Morris developed not only as a craftsman but also as a player.

During the 1840s the pair regularly competed together, forming a formidable foursomes partnership, and in 1849 they played a famous challenge match against the Dunn twins from Mussleburgh. Battle took place over three courses – Mussleburgh, North Berwick and St. Andrews – with the winning team pocketing a healthy £400. Both sides won on their home courses meaning honours were even heading into the final, neutral venue at North Berwick. Morris and Robertson were four down with eight holes to play but showed typical determination to fight back and remarkably they closed out the match on the final green.

But, sadly, after almost a decade together their relationship ended on a sour note. Robertson had resisted the trend towards manufacturing more durable, gutty golf balls in favour of the age-old, handmade feathery versions. So strongly did he resent the impact of the new ball (it offered greater distance and a smoother roll on the greens) that when Old Tom played in a match using a gutty

BELOW
The remote course of Machriha was designed by Old Tom Morris seen here in 1927.

Robertson was outraged. The two men fell out spectacularly and their differences remained forever irreconcilable.

In 1851 Old Tom moved from St. Andrews to Prestwick, accepting a job as 'custodian of the links'. His role involved all the responsibilities expected of a modern day club professional, with the added obligation of grooming the 12-hole course – all for 15 shillings per week. This meant he was able to continue making clubs and balls, as well as playing regularly with members.

And it was on the links at Prestwick that the Open Championship was born in 1860. With a field of just eight competitors, the first Open was a modest affair that was squeezed into the autumn schedule at Prestwick – to the frustration of many of the members. Morris was one of the game's leading players with an intimate knowledge of the Prestwick layout but the inaugural Championship was won by his great rival from Musselburgh, Willie Park. However, twelve months later Old Tom captured his first Open victory, winning the 1861 event with a 36-hole total of 163 – 11 shots better than Park's score the previous year.

Morris was an ever present at the Open until 1896 winning the title on four occasions through the 1860s. Later, he continued to support the Championship through its evolution from a small event played over 36 holes to the four-round format with scores of strong competitors, played on a cluster of great courses. The

exciting international event that we love today evolved through the ardent support of its'
first competitors – men such as Old Tom Morris.

After 14 years working at Prestwick Morris eventually returned to St. Andrews in 1865.
As well as fulfilling his role as custodian of the links Old Tom also turned his hand to
course design and his unique touch can be seen on layouts such as Carnoustie, Lahinch,
Royal Dornoch, Nairn and Royal County Down. By adding new courses to the British
landscape he helped the game become more accessible and his vision for a links
challenge doubtless influenced the great course designers that followed him.

By the time Old Tom Morris died in 1908 golf had grown into a popular sport for the
masses. The Open Championship was established as the flagship event, each year
crowning another genuine superstar. The influence of Old Tom through the early
evolution of the game was invaluable. His role as the first club professional, his support
of the Open Championship and his golf course architecture have left a lasting legacy, a
crucial chapter in the history of the game.

The Little Book of **GOLF** LEGENDS

YOUNGTOM
MORRIS

Born: St. Andrews, Scotland 1851
Died: December 25th, 1875
Open: Winner in 1868, 1869, 1870, 1872

Through the 1860s and 70s, Young Tom Morris was golf's star attraction, a young prodigy who seemed more at home on the course than anyone before him, including his father. He was the outstanding talent of his time and despite dying at the tender age of 24, became a crucial figure in the evolution of the Open Championship.

When Young Tom Morris was born in St. Andrews in 1851 golf was an emerging game played by a handful of people on a handful of courses. But for Young Tom, growing up near the 12-hole links at Prestwick under the guidance of his father – the game's first professional, golf was in his blood.

Young Tom quickly developed a sound technique to ally his natural mental fortitude and by the age of 13 was already emerging as a player of serious note. In 1864, he played a challenge match in Perth against a talented local by the name of William Greig. A sizeable crowd turned out to watch Young Tom defeat his skillful opponent.

This performance confirmed that, even as a boy, he was one of the best players in the country and just three years later in 1867 he made his Open debut. His father may have taken the title that year – his fourth and final victory – but Young Tom finished a highly commendable fourth. This early experience proved invaluable and Young Tom returned the following year to make his mark.

Still in its infancy, the Open was played each year at Prestwick attracting small fields of around 15 players that comprised of professionals and various capable members of established golf clubs. The man with the lowest score after three 12-hole rounds was crowned champion and received an ostentatious red leather Moroccan belt that that was decorated with silver buckles.

In 1868, Young Tom Morris triumphed over 12 of the best players of the day (including his father) – it was a victory that marked the beginning of his reign. Aged just 17 at the time, he remains the youngest player ever to have won the Open, a record that looks set to last forever.

The following year pitted father and son against each other in a final round dual as the rest of the field lagged helplessly behind (Bob Kirk finished third, some 11 strokes shy of the winning total). Neither player could claim the advantage of knowing more about the intricacies of the course and it was Young Tom who prevailed by three shots.

By this time, Young Tom Morris was at the height of his powers (he had a hole-in-one on the eighth hole of his opening round) and many other competitors believed that he

was simply unbeatable. He duly completed a hat-trick of victories in 1870, defeating his great friend Davie Strath by 12 shots. His winning total of 149 was a record for the three round format that remained unbeaten (the Open became 72 holes in 1891).

The tournament organisers had previously decreed that if a player won the event three times, he was entitled to keep the prize. Young Tom accepted the Moroccan belt and without a trophy to fight for the following year, there was no championship.

In 1872 the members at Prestwick decided that for the Championship to continue it needed additional support from the R&A and the Honourable Company of Edinburgh Golfers. Between them they would pick up the bill for a new trophy. Sadly for Young Tom, who won the Open for the fourth time that year, no trophy had yet been commissioned.

So the iconic image that represents our great championship – the Claret Jug – was born in 1873 when the Open moved from Prestwick for the first time and headed for St. Andrews. But just as Young

Tom Morris appeared to be invincible, destined to make the Claret Jug his own, his reign came to an end. His triumph of 1872 was his last – the following three Opens were won by Tom Kidd and Willie and Mungo Park.

In 1875 Young Tom played a challenge match with his father against Willie and Mungo Park at Mussleburgh. As he walked off the final green he was handed a telegram explaining that his wife was experiencing complications during the birth of their first child. Young Tom and his father immediately set sail for St. Andrews but the news on their arrival was not good – both wife and child were dead.

This tragedy clearly rocked Young Tom and returning to St. Andrews to live with his parents, he played very little golf for the remainder of the year. Many believe that his death on Christmas Day in 1895 was the result of a broken heart despite the more scientific medical opinion that sited pneumonia.

By 1872 Young Tom Morris was golf's first real superstar. His impeccable ball striking was matched by a deadly putting stroke – an exciting formula that provoked a new level of interest in the game. And were it not for his hat-trick of victories from 1868 to 1870, the famous Claret Jug may never have been born!

LEFT
The Open Golf Championships entrants for 1865, featuring Young Tom Morris (2nd from top left) and to the immediate right Old Tom Morris.

FAR LEFT
Father and son. Young Tom pictured with his dad Old Tom.

BYRON
NELSON

Born: Waxahachie, Texas February 4, 1912
Turned professional: 1932
Masters: Winner in 1937, 1942
US Open: Winner in 1939
Open: 5th in 1937
USPGA: Winner in 1940, 1945
Ryder Cup record: Member of 2 US
teams (1937, 1947). Played 4, Won 3,
Lost 1. Captain in 1965

In 1945, Byron Nelson set a staggering record by winning 11 consecutive tournaments. In one single year his achievements, including 19 tournament victories at a stroke average of 68.83, reveal a gifted man at the very peak of his powers and it was a brief period of total domination that no other player has come close to matching. But there was one crucial component missing from Nelson's psychological make-up – he lacked the same determination that drove other great players to compete year after year and exceed his record of five major victories. His gruelling 1945 tournament schedule took its toll on Nelson and at the end of the season he retired, aged 34.

BELOW
Byron Nelson watches golfers in his own Byron Nelson Golf Classic.

Byron Nelson grew up within close proximity of the golf course at the Glen Garden Club in Texas and by the age of 10, he was already earning a wage as a caddie. An ideal occupation for an energetic young boy, Nelson was joined in the caddie ranks at Glen Garden by none other than Ben Hogan. Through their early years the two formed a healthy and friendly rivalry on the course that helped them both develop as strong competitors, sustaining their interest in the game. Throughout the 1930s and 40s Nelson's career progressed ahead of Hogan's and after victory in the 1930 South West Amateur Championship had confirmed that a career in golf could be lucrative, Nelson graduated to the professional ranks in 1932.

His debut season on Tour however, was a bitter disappointment. The success he craved never materialised and for a brief period Nelson sought an alternative career away from the golf course, in the oil business. But when the dust settled on his frustrating start as a tournament golfer, he devoted himself to the game. In 1934 some respectable finishes boosted his finances and enabled him to secure a job as an assistant professional at the Ridgewood Club in New Jersey. Nelson's breakthrough year on Tour came in 1936 – he finished ninth on the moneylist and

captured his first significant title, the Metropolitan Open.

Byron Nelson won the first of his five major titles in 1937 at the age of 26. With seven holes left to play at Augusta, he was trailing Ralph Guldahl by four shots. But the infamous risk and reward back nine provided a stunning twist, starting at the par-3 12th. As Nelson birdied, Guldahl found water to score a double bogey five. Sensing that his more experienced opponent was feeling the heat, Nelson bravely attacked the par-5 13th, hitting the green in two. He duly converted his eagle putt and as Guldahl registered a bogey six, Nelson was suddenly sitting proud at the head of the field. He clung on to the lead to take the title with a four round total of 283.

Further US Tour victories followed in 1938 but Nelson was ill at ease with his own game. He believed that to build on this early success his rather loose technique needed tightening. So he set about remodelling his swing and he did not have to wait long for this important decision to be vindicated. He won his only US Open title in 1939, at the expense of one of his great rivals, Sam Snead. Standing on the final tee, Snead needed a par five to take the title but his golf disintegrated and he closed with a devastating eight. This left Nelson, Craig Wood and Denny Shute to fight for the honours in extra time. After 18 holes, Nelson and Wood were

LEFT
Byron Nelson –
honorary starter,
plays from the
1st tee on the
opening day of
the Masters, 1994.

FAR LEFT
Nelson competing in
the 1937 Ryder Cup
at Royal Birkdale.

tied on 69 with Shute eliminated after a score of 76. Another 18 holes were needed to separate Nelson from Wood, 70 to 73.

Byron Nelson was adept at imposing his will on his opponents as his record in the USPGA reveals. He reached five finals in six years, winning twice during this period. His mental strength was also crucial in capturing the 1942 US Masters. After four rounds, Hogan and Nelson were locked on a total of 280. In an exciting play-off, the two laid on a shotmaking masterclass, with Nelson pipping his great rival by one shot after a sparkling 69.

Between 1939 and 1945, many of the world's top golfers including Sam Snead and Ben Hogan were involved in military service. Nelson however, suffered from haemophilia and was exempt from fighting in the armed forces. Sadly for Nelson, his most spectacular run of form coincided with the closing stages of World War II and with some big names missing, his numerous, emphatic victories were somewhat devalued. In 1945, his aggregate tournament score was an incredible 113 under par, he won $66,000 and his average winning margin was over six shots. His 19 tournament victories included a second USPGA Championship at Dayton, Ohio.

For Nelson, this incredible year brought him all the success he desired. Having journeyed across the length and bredth of America, he was exhausted and with his trophy cabinet bulging, he decided to retire the following year.

Byron Nelson's achievements will forever assure him a place among the game's elite. The fact that he retired at the age of 34, just as most golfers are reaching their prime, leaves a question mark over just what he might have accomplished had he the natural drive of a Nick Faldo or a Jack Nicklaus.

JACK**NICKLAUS**

Born: Columbus, Ohio January 21, 1940
Turned professional: 1962
Masters: Winner in 1963, 1965, 1966, 1972, 1975, 1986
US Open: Winner in 1962, 1967, 1972, 1980
Open: Winner in 1966, 1970, 1978
USPGA: Winner in 1963, 1971, 1973, 1975, 1980
Ryder Cup record: Member of 6 US teams (1969, 1971, 1973, 1975, 1977, 1981). Played 28, Won 17, Lost 8, Halved 3. Captain in 1983 and 1987

The problem with any discussion about the greatest golfers of all time is that it is impossible to compare players of different generations. Debating whether Hogan would have beaten Ballesteros, or if Jones was a more talented ball striker than Woods is interesting, but ultimately futile. The only quantifiable measure of a golfer's ability lies in his list of achievements, and this is where Jack Nicklaus stands proudly above the rest. For some, crossing the winning line requires the wrestling of mental demons but for Nicklaus it was a natural progression. Quite simply, he was an instinctive winner whose 18 major victories have become the yardstick by which greatness is now measured.

BELOW
Nicklaus in action at
the Open in 1972.

It was evident from an early age that Jack Nicklaus had a special talent for the game. Having been introduced to golf by his father at the age of 10 young Nicklaus was recording scores in the 70s just two years later. He quickly grasped many of the key fundamentals under the tutelage of Jack Grout, the professional at Scioto Country Club in Ohio. Importantly, Grout never tempered the hard-hitting instincts of his star pupil and even as a teenager Nicklaus was notorious for his powerful game. By the age of 16 he was winning state amateur titles and was good enough to earn a place in the field for the US Amateur. He was a crucial member of the winning American Walker Cup team in 1959 and the following year finished second in the US Open, two shots behind Arnold Palmer. It was clear that Nicklaus was a major champion in the making and after winning his second US Amateur title in 1961, he turned pro.

The foundation laid by a relatively long and successful amateur career paid off during his first year in the paid ranks as he won the US Open at Oakmont. At this time Arnold Palmer was the best player in the world and the crowd adored his dynamic gameplan and easy-going character. Conversely, Nicklaus seemed to have a cocky, bullish character to match his stocky physique. When the two men went

head-to-head in a play-off for the 1962 US Open it was clear who the public were rooting for. But Nicklaus confirmed his hype, beating his esteemed opponent by three shots.

Nicklaus remained an unpopular winner for some time but as he matured into his late 20s he suddenly relaxed his public persona. He lost weight, grew his hair and started wearing more fashionable clothes – changes that did not go unnoticed by the public – and his popularity grew quickly.

Through the 60s and 70s Nicklaus consistently challenged for and won major honours. When he captured the 1966 Open at Muirfield, he became only the fourth man to complete a Grand Slam – he was just 26 years old. But it wasn't until the 70s that "The Golden Bear" reached his peak, winning seven majors between 1970 and 1975. His career at the highest level continued well into the next decade too, his fifth and final Green Jacket arriving in 1986. Despite experiencing a few relatively barren years on Tour the 46-year-old was still a threat when the biggest prizes were on offer. By making one of his trademark final round charges he accelerated past Greg Norman and Tom Kite to win by a single shot.

In a career filled with so many magnificent successes it might seem strange to focus on his failures but they provide an

interesting insight into the character of Jack Nicklaus. After losing an epic battle with Tom Watson in the sunshine at Turnberry during the 1977 Open Nicklaus walked off the final green with his arm around his opponent, offering his congratulations. In the Ryder Cup of 1969 he conceded a short but missable putt on the final green of his crucial singles match against Tony Jacklin (despite having lost to the same man in the morning matches). Nicklaus did not want to see his great rival hand America the Cup by missing from close range. The match was shared and so was the Ryder Cup, ending a decade of US domination in the event. Not even Jack Nicklaus could win them all but it became clear that he was just as gracious in defeat as he was in victory.

By the end of his career, Jack Nicklaus had completed the Grand Slam three times over. There were also countless near misses as the likes of Player, Trevino and Watson held his predictably fierce challenges at bay. Since retiring from the Tour Nicklaus has become a leading figure in golf course architecture. Highly regarded layouts such as Muirfield Village, Castle Pines and Valhalla bear his vision of long carries, well-positioned bunkers and vastly undulating greens. But regardless of his considerable achievements off the course Jack Nicklaus will forever be remembered for a breathtaking game that simply bore no sign of weakness.

FAR LEFT
Jack Nicklaus with the Open trophy in 1978, St. Andrews.

MIDDLE
The Swilcan Bridge, at St. Andrews where Jack made an emotional farewell to the Open.

BELOW
Nicklaus wins the Masters aged 46 in 1986.

JOSÉMARÍA**OLAZÁBAL**

Born: Fuenterrabia, Spain February 5, 1966

Turned professional: 1985

Masters: Winner in 1994, 1999

US Open: Tied 8th in 1990 and 1991

Open: 3rd in 1992

USPGA: Tied 4th in 2000

Ryder Cup record: Member of 6 European teams
(1987, 1989, 1991, 1993, 1997, 1999). Played 28, Won 15,
Lost 8, Halved 5

The career of José María Olazábal was divided into two distinct phases by a mysterious foot injury that threatened to leave him unable to walk. During an 18-month hiatus from competitive action his world ranking plummeted from ninth to 225th. But Olazábal's game was built on a natural aptitude for clean ball striking and a deft touch around the greens, so when he returned to fitness in 1997 few doubted that he was capable of scaling previous heights. With two majors, 25 Tour titles and six Ryder Cup appearances to his name, José María Olazábal has been one of the world's most dangerous competitors for the last two decades.

BELOW
Olazábal plays from a bunker during the World MatchPlay at Wentworth, 2005.

The Olazábal family home is situated within 100 yards of the 9th green at the Real San Sebastian Golf Club in Northern Spain. Both his father and grandfather worked for a modest wage as greenkeepers, enabling José María to pick up the game at an early age. But unlike fellow Spaniard, Seve Ballesteros who had graduated from caddie to professional by the age of 16 Olazábal was able to develop his game through a long and successful amateur career. In 1983 he captured both Italian and Spanish Amateur Championships as well as the British Boys title. Then in 1984, at the age of 18 he defeated Colin Montgomerie in the final of the British Amateur by 5&4 at Formby. After winning the British Youths title the following year he decided to turn professional and immediately qualified to play on the European Tour.

Being one of the least experienced members on Tour did not phase José María as he was accustomed to success. In his debut season he notched victories at the European Masters and Sanyo Open to finish second on the order of merit. Between 1986 and 1994, Olazábal won 15 times on the European Tour and twice in America. He was emerging as a top class player desperately looking for his first major title.

The course at Augusta National could have been designed with José María's game in mind. Wide fairways flanked by minimal

amounts of rough forgive the odd errant tee shot while slick, undulating greens push short game skills to the limit. Throughout his career Olazábal has struggled to tame his driver but from the fairway his approach play remains deadly and his short game is always one of the best on Tour. Having come close to winning the Green Jacket in 1991, when Ian Woosnam pipped him by a single stroke, it was clear that the Masters represented his best chance of breaking into the major winner's circle. He duly did so in 1994 after an epic battle with American, Tom Lehman. The title was decided on the par-5 15th when Olazábal holed a 30ft eagle putt from the fringe. Lehman was closer to the hole than his challenger in two but missed his eagle putt and the 28-year-old Spaniard coasted to a two shot victory. Then in 1999 he continued a rich vein of European success in the Masters by holding off a stiff challenge from Greg Norman and Davis Love to win by two once again.

José María Olazábal won the 1994 Masters despite feeling a niggling pain in his feet. As he played through the remainder of the season the problem got progressively worse until he could barely walk. At the end of the year, medical advice sighted

rheumatoid arthritis but the diagnosis was wrong and the subsequent operation failed to rectify the problem. Unable to walk, let alone play golf during 1996, Olazábal sought an alternative opinion and finally, a German doctor discovered that he was suffering from a spinal hernia. Olazábal battled back to fitness through a rigorous and painful regime that combined exercise with physiotherapy. He returned to the European Tour in time for the 1997 Dubai Desert Classic and two weeks later completed a sensational comeback by winning the Turespana Masters Open de Canaria.

The injury to his feet forced him to pull out of the 1995 Ryder Cup at Oak Hill, but the Spaniard has still amassed six appearances in his career to date, winning 17½ points. His formidable partnership with Seve Ballesteros was crucial in the first ever European victory on American soil in 1987 – they won three of four matches together. In total the Spaniards played in four Ryder Cups, and their partnership yielded a mighty 12 points. They added flair to the European team and injected some genuine passion into the event.

When José María Olazábal reached his peak in the 1990s, he was a regular winner with a fast, compact swing and an unerring putting stroke. His two Green Jackets are a monument to his innate ability to raise his game under intense pressure. Now aged 40, he remains one of the most dangerous and popular European competitors on Tour.

ARNOLD
PALMER

Born: Latrobe, Pennsylvania September 10, 1929
Turned professional: 1954
Masters: Winner in 1958, 1960, 1962, 1964
US Open: Winner in 1960
Open: Winner in 1961, 1962
USPGA: Winner in 1962, 1972
Ryder Cup record: Member of 6 US teams (1961, 1963, 1965, 1967, 1971, 1973). Played 32, Won 22, Lost 8, Halved 2. Captain in 1963 and 1975

Golf's graduation from a minority sport to a global game in which those at the pinnacle can expect to become multi-millionaires was given a mighty push by the swashbuckling Arnold Palmer. His gung-ho gameplan, immense skill and friendly demeanour were all captured on television and he became the all American hero who did more to popularise the sport than any other player on this list. Such was the impact of "The King" on the golfing world that playing into his 70s he still attracted enormous crowds desperate to pay their respects.

Much like Young Tom Morris over 75 years before Arnold Palmer grew up with golf in his blood. His father, Deacon, left his job as a steel miner in Pennsylvania to become a golf professional at a small local club, ensuring that his young son would have a firm foothold within the game. But unlike Jack Nicklaus and Gary Player, Palmer's progression into professionalism was far less smooth. Despite being the top-ranked player at Wake Forest College Palmer spent three years in the US coastguards and even tried his hand as a salesman before winning the US Amateur in 1954 and settling on a future in golf.

When Palmer did finally emerge as a serious competitor Ben Hogan was the fading super power in the American game. His major victories of 1953 were to be his last and nobody had captured the public's imagination in quite the same way until Palmer swept to victory in the 1958 Masters. Typically, he left his final round charge to the very last minute, making birdies at the last two holes to pip Doug Ford and Jack Hawkins.

Then in 1960, after winning his second Masters title, Palmer faced a seven shot deficit heading into the final round of the US Open at Cherry Hills in Denver. More importantly there were also 12 highly talented players between himself and leader, Mike Souchak. The tempo for the day was set early on as Palmer made four birdies on the first four holes and reached the turn in just 30 blows.

The cavalier style of this triumph (including an eagle on the 13th) endeared

BELOW
Palmer at the 1994 US Open plays out the infamous 'church pews' bunker, Oakmont.

him to the press and public and he went on to appear on the front cover of Sports Illustrated 12 times, as well as becoming one of the few sportsmen to make it onto the front cover of Time magazine.

But it wasn't just in the States that Palmer was capturing the public's imagination. He won our Open Championship twice and in 1961, at Royal Birkdale, he laid on a particularly virtuoso display. With strong winds buffeting the Lancashire coastline only the purest ball strikers were able to compete and Palmer won the event by a single shot from Dai Rees. Despite the strength of the wind Palmer's strategy was typically bullish. On the par-5 15th during the final round he forced his second shot from deep rough onto the green, a shot that very few others would have even considered. His victory broke the Thompson/Locke era of domination, re-awakening a strong American challenge and adding some much-needed impetus to the Championship. The British public recognised the importance of Palmer's sudden impact and he remains a popular figure on this side of the Atlantic.

On the course, Arnold Palmer lived life on the brink but having such a bold gameplan is a double-edged sword and his defeats were often just as spectacular as his victories. Only three months before his triumph at Birkdale Palmer walked up the

final fairway at Augusta needing a par-4 to win the Masters. He caught the bunker to the right of the green, thinned his next shot over the other side of the putting surface and then chipped and two putted for a double bogey six. Palmer had handed Gary Player his first Green Jacket on a plate. Then at Olympic Fields, during the US Open of 1966, Palmer threw away a six-shot lead over Billy Casper. He appeared in total control heading into the final few holes but recorded a disastrous run of figures that included a six on the 16th, where he tried to hit a 3-iron from deep rough (the triumphant memories of Royal Birkdale were clearly still fresh in his mind). He lost the subsequent play-off by four shots and never did manage to add to his major tally of eight.

Arnold Palmer enriched the game with moments of genuine theatre that unfolded in front of television cameras to growing audiences. He had a common touch and fallibility that brought him closer to the people who paid to watch him play. These qualities meant that when he won it seemed heroic and when he lost, everyone shared in his despair.

FAR LEFT
Palmer at Royal Birkdale in 1961, where he won his first Open title.

MIDDLE
Palmer in Ryder Cup action, 1973.

BELOW
Arnold Palmer stands next to a plaque unveiled in his honour at the 1995 Masters.

GARY
PLAYER

Born: Johannesburg, South Africa November 1, 1935
Turned professional: 1953
Masters: Winner in 1961, 1974, 1978
US Open: Winner in 1965
Open: Winner in 1959, 1968, 1974
USPGA: Winner in 1962, 1972

Self-belief is a powerful asset and **Gary Player** was a master of positive thinking. Without considering anything but the perfect outcome he imposed his will on the course and his opponent. By also working tirelessly on his game and maintaining his peak physical condition Player enjoyed four decades at the highest level. And in the style of all the great South African golfers he travelled extensively, confident that his game would prevail on any course in the world.

Born in Johannesburg in 1935 Gary Player was just six years old when his mother died of cancer. Despite his tender years this tragedy left an indelible mark on the young man as his father, a worker in a gold mine, was left to care and provide for the family. It was Player's father who introduced Gary to the game at the age of 15, and he soon became hooked.

Virginia Park in Johannesburg was the venue for his initial golfing education and under the guidance of the head professional Jock Vewery – Player soon developed a respectable game. Even as a teenager, he had the dedication and discipline to work hard and this maturity enabled him to secure a job as Vewery's assistant before graduating to head professional at Killarney Golf Club. Both placements offered a secure living in Johannesburg albeit without the buzz of competitive golf. Player realised that to fulfil his ambition of golfing for a living he needed to leave South Africa. So aged 19, and without any serious success behind him, Player travelled to Britain to pursue his career as a tournament professional.

At first, Player struggled as tournament golf exposed his developing game and many of his fellow competitors felt that his grip was too strong and his backswing too flat. They made it known that he didn't have the mechanics to compete and advised him to return to his comfortable life as a teaching pro in South Africa. Unperturbed, Player continued to graft as hard as ever and in 1956 he won an important Dunlop sponsored event at Sunningdale.

The following year he crossed the Atlantic to pit his game against the likes of

Arnold Palmer and Billy Casper on the US Tour. In 1958 he won the Kentucky Open, adding his name to a rare list of internationals to triumph on American soil. Player was gaining recognition as a serious force and his first major victory arrived at Muirfield in 1959. Aged just 22, he became the second South African to win the Open Championship.

Further victories in the Masters (1961) and the USPGA (1962) quickly followed, leaving the US Open as the missing leg of the Grand Slam. But in 1965 he became the third golfer in history to have won all four majors after winning a tight play-off with Kel Nagl. In an extraordinary act of generosity, he donated his $26,000 winner's cheque to the USGA for investment in a cancer charity and junior golf.

Gary Player was a gritty competitor and throughout his career he excelled in the head-to-head format, winning the World Matchplay Championship five times. In 1967 he won an incredible match against Tony Lema despite facing a seven hole deficit at the half way stage. Then on his way to claiming the 1968 title he met Tony Jacklin in the semi-final. Player missed a short putt on the 36th hole to win the match and certain members of the partisan crowd could be heard cheering. At the first play-off hole both men were faced with tricky putts for par and, this time, some of Jacklin's fans disturbed Player just as he was about to strike his crucial putt. The South African may have been seething but he composed himself and waited for the

The Little Book of **GOLF** LEGENDS

crowd to settle down before holing out and piling the pressure on his opponent. Jacklin duly missed his short putt and the match was over.

As this episode highlights, Gary Player was undoubtedly one of the toughest competitors the game has ever seen. Dressed in black, he appeared utterly single-minded in his determination to win. By paying close attention to his diet and taking regular, strenuous exercise Player was also able to compete at the highest level well into his 40s. In fact, his last major triumph came at the Masters in 1978 when he was 42. Heading into the final round Player was seven shots adrift of the leader Hubert Green with other big names such as Nicklaus, Ballesteros, Watson and Trevino also in the hunt. But despite the pedigree of his younger opponents it was Player who accelerated to the top of the leaderboard shooting a remarkable 30 for the last nine holes to complete a sparkling round of 64.

Gary Player's risky decision to leave a comfortable life in South Africa and follow in the footsteps of Bobby Locke paid off because he would never accept failure. His positive mental outlook was perhaps his greatest asset, enabling him to compete consistently in four separate decades and become one of the few to capture golf's four greatest prizes.

ABOVE

Gary Player in action on the 18th tee at the 2000 US Masters.

FAR LEFT

Gary Player kisses the Open trophy on his third win in 1974.

GENE**SARAZEN**

Born: New York February 27, 1902
Died: May 13, 1999
Turned professional: 1920
Masters: Winner in 1935
US Open: Winner in 1922, 1932
Open: Winner in 1932
USPGA: Winner in 1922, 1923, 1933
Ryder Cup record: Member of 6 US teams
(1927, 1929, 1931, 1933, 1935, 1937). Played 12,
Won 7, Lost 2, Halved 3

When Gene Sarazen won the Masters in 1935 he became the first golfer to complete the Grand Slam. At just 5ft 3ins tall Sarazen was a diminutive figure with an intense determination that drove his career for over half a century. His list of triumphs dates back to the US Open of 1922, and he remained competitive into his 70s. Sarazen's story is one that reveals hard graft and skill in equal measures.

Sarazen's willingness to make the most of his natural talent as a golfer can be traced back to his early years, growing up in Harrison, New York. Born Eugeni Sarazani in 1902, he was the son of Italian immigrants and his upbringing was far from privileged. By the age of eight, he was caddying at a local country club to supplement the family income. He left school at 15 and moved with his family to Connecticut where he worked as an apprentice in a factory. Labouring in difficult conditions Sarazen contracted pleurisy and his doctor recommended that he should work outside to accelerate his recuperation. He soon found a job at Brooklawn Country Club where his duties included making clubs and generally helping the resident professional.

By 17 he had changed his name to the more American sounding "Gene" and was earning his wage as an assistant professional. When he arrived at the Skokie Country Club, Illinois, to compete in the 1922 US Open he was an unknown 20-year-old but despite his tender years and relative inexperience, Sarazen became the first

player to break 70 in the final round to win. His sparkling 68 included a birdie on the final hole after hitting his second shot approach to the par-5 with a driver. The exciting and fearless fashion of his first major victory propelled Sarazen into the limelight and later that year he won the US PGA to kick-start his career at the top level with an incredible bang.

In 1923 Sarazen won the USPGA for the second time, but this would be his last major triumph until the Open of 1932. This hiatus divides his record into two distinct phases and can be blamed on two

factors – the emergence of Bobby Jones and a growing concern over his technique. Sarazen was a small man with a compact swing that lacked the rhythmic beauty of his great contemporary. He employed an interlocking hold and his left thumb had a tendency to fly away from the grip during the swing. Despite some respectable results during a period in which he worked hard to rectify the faults, Sarazen lacked the self-confidence to succeed under intense pressure.

He finally returned to the winner's circle in 1932 with victory at the Open by an emphatic five shots over fellow American Macdonald Smith. His four round total of 283 was a record that remained unbeaten until Bobby Locke scored 279 at Troon in 1950. Sarazen then crossed the Atlantic to claim the US Open crown at Fresh Meadow in New York. In keeping with the style of his victory 10 years earlier he shot 66 on the final day to win by three, playing the final 28 holes in a staggering 100 shots.

Sarazen's seventh and final major title came in 1935 at the US Masters, where his influence over the back nine helped create its modern day reputation for being the most dangerous stretch in the game. Standing on the par-5 15th tee of his final round, Sarazen was three shots behind an imperious Craig Wood. He followed a long, straight drive with a 4-wood approach that found the bottom of the cup.

This incredible albatross enabled Sarazen to force a play-off that he eventually won by five strokes.

The Masters of 1935 was Sarazen's last great triumph although he remained a serious competitor for another four decades. During the Open of 1973 at Troon, (50 years after his debut in the event) he scored a hole-in-one at the 8th on his way to shooting an impressive round of 79.

Like many of his contemporaries, Sarazen's achievements stretched beyond competition, and he is credited with the design of the modern sand wedge after he realised that by building up the sole, the clubhead would maintain its momentum as it bounced through sand. This discovery suddenly made bunker shots an easier proposition as players could hit aggressively behind the ball and still expect to see it emerge onto the green. He also presented the popular television show, "Shell's Wonderful World of Golf" that brought many of the game's great players together in head-to-head battles. By the time of his death in 1999 at the age of 97, Gene Sarazen had left an indelible mark on the game he cherished.

ABOVE
Sarazen in Ryder Cup action, 1929.

FAR LEFT
Gene Sarazen with the Open trophy in 1932.

VIJAY**SINGH**

Born: Lautoke, Fiji February 22, 1963
Turned professional: 1982
Masters: Winner in 2000
US Open: Tied 3rd in 1999
Open: Tied 2nd in 2003
USPGA: Winner in 1998, 2004

On September 6th, 2004, 41-year-old Vijay Singh won the Deutsche Bank
Championship in Boston and ended Tiger Woods' 264-week reign as the best golfer
in the world. He remains the only player to have consistently challenged Woods,
never doubting his ability to beat his great opponent when it really mattered. His
achievements, including three major championships, have been founded on a
combination of natural talent and old-fashioned hard graft. And it is this work ethic
that enabled Singh to leave his native Fiji with a game good enough to compete
against high caliber fields all around the world.

BELOW
Singh at the US
Masters 2006.

When Vijay Singh turned professional in 1982 he knew that success on the Asian Tour
would have to come thick and, more importantly, fast to make it as a player. Growing up
in Nadi, Fiji, Singh did not have the sort of structured golfing education afforded to
players in the American university system. Instead, his father, an airplane technician and
part-time golf instructor, was responsible for Singh's development as a player and
encouraged his son to pursue his early infatuation with the game. So at the age of 19
Singh set about travelling through Asia scraping a living on Tour. His breakthrough
victory came two years later at the Malaysian PGA. This win confirmed the Fijian's talent
and finally vindicated his brave decision to play competitively for a living.

Despite the consistent success that followed, Singh's ascent to the major Tours
proved to be a difficult journey. At the 1985
Indonesian Open he was accused of
altering the score on his card and despite
professing his innocence was suspended
from the Asian Tour for two years. For a
player beginning to make his mark this was
a bitter blow as he was forced to retire to
Borneo to become a club professional. But
the financial security of a steady job enabled
Singh to save enough money to resurrect his
career and he did not have to wait long for
success. On his return he won the 1988
Nigerian Open and soon qualified to
compete on the European Tour.

Over the next four years Singh was a regular winner in Europe and in 1993 he graduated to the US Tour. Having captured the Buick Classic, defeating Mark Wiebe in a play-off, Singh was named PGA Tour Rookie of the Year. Back and neck injuries may have hampered his progress the following season but facing fierce competition week after week was making the Fijian a resolute competitor.

In 1998, aged 35, Vijay Singh became a major winner. The venue for the USPGA Championship was the 6,906-yard, par 70 layout at Sahalee in Seattle. Throughout the week Singh's game was a model of consistency and he added scores of 66, 67 and 68 to his opening round of 70 to take the title by two shots from American Steve Stricker. Two years later he picked up the Green Jacket, defeating Ernie Els by three shots after a spectacular final round 69.

Moving towards his 40s Vijay Singh could have been forgiven for relaxing the intensive practice regime that had become his trademark, but he continued to work just as hard as ever to close the gap between himself and Tiger Woods. His devotion paid off spectacularly in 2003 when he recorded a staggering 18 top 10 finishes, including four tournament victories. This amazing run coincided with a dip

in form from Woods and the Fijian ended the season on top of the moneylist, having won almost $1 million more than his great rival.

But the glory of 2003 was just a teaser for what was about to unfold. He won nine times in 2004, including his second USPGA Championship in a play-off against Chris DiMarco and Justin Leonard at Whistling Straits. The 42-year-old amassed over $10 million in prize money and, crucially, took Tiger's world number one crown. For the first time in seven years there was a new name at the top of the golfing world.

But through this period of domination controversy was never far away and Singh was heavily criticised in all areas of the media. In 2003, Annika Sorenstam accepted an invitation to play on the PGA Tour, much to Singh's frustration. He felt that she was taking the place of a journeyman player trying to make a living and his rash comments were construed by many as sexist. Then there is the prickly relationship between himself and Woods which was sparked at the President's Cup of 2000 when Singh's caddie wore a baseball cap that read, "Tiger who?" Woods felt this to be disrespectful and as the Fijian passed the American in the world rankings their encounters remained hostile.

And yet despite these controversies, Singh commands respect for making the most of his God-given talent and emerging from the pack to become the only successful challenger to the great Tiger Woods.

SAM**SNEAD**

Born: Hot Springs, Virginia May 27 1912
Died: May 23, 2002
Turned professional: 1934
Masters: Winner in 1949, 1952, 1954
US Open: 2nd in 1932, 1947, 1953
Open: Winner in 1946
USPGA: Winner in 1942, 1949, 1951
Ryder Cup record: Member of 7 US teams (1937, 1947, 1949, 1951, 1953, 1955, 1959). Played 13, Won 10, Lost 2, Halved 1. Captain in 1951, 1959, 1969

The age-old golfing proverb 'it's not how but how many', which places low scores above perfect methods, is sound advice. However, given the choice any golfer would love to swing with the same brand of power and elegance that became the signature of Samuel Jackson Snead. His instinctively smooth style has led many to believe that the man from Virginia was, in fact, the most talented the sport has ever seen. But whilst his record of seven major championships remains a glorious testament to his great ability, it falls some way short of the achievements of Nicklaus, Palmer, Hogan and Woods. Despite his immense talent (he was the first player to shoot 59 in competition) "Slamming Sam's" Achilles heel was his mental application.

Sam Snead was born in May 1912 near the town of Hot Springs in the backwaters of Virginia. His family owned a small plot of land and Snead, along with his five brothers, would lend his hand to various odd jobs including milling and chicken tending. At school he had a reputation as a talented sportsman, playing baseball, basketball and football to a decent standard. But it was only when he left full-time education and secured a job working at his local course that he started playing golf regularly. Through these early years Snead developed his own unique style and quickly emerged as a player of serious note. In fact, the strength of his performances led to a move to the wealthier Greenbrier Club at White Sulpher Springs. Here his education as a player continued as he caddied for, and then taught, the club's members. Snead clearly made a serious impact on the Greenbrier regulars as in 1936 they clubbed together to finance his attempts to make it on Tour.

BELOW

Honorary starter Sam Snead at the 2002 Masters.

With just $300 to his name he knew that to continue competing he would have to record some top finishes, and fast. He duly won the Oakland Open on his third start, pocketing a cheque for $1,200 in the process.

This kick-started a professional career that spanned an incredible six decades, during which time Snead was a regular

winner. He claimed his first major title in 1942 at the USPGA, which at the time was a matchplay championship, defeating Jim Turnesa in the final by 2&1.

His next major victory came at St. Andrews in the Open of 1946. Throughout his career Snead competed very few times outside America and only travelled to play in the Open on three occasions. In 1937 he finished tied 11th at Carnoustie and when he returned to the Fife coast

nine years later was relatively green in the intricacies of Scottish seaside golf. And yet despite this inexperience, and a burning dislike for the course, he prevailed by four strokes in typically strong winds, proving his natural class. But sadly for the British public he only made one more appearance in the Open, an unremarkable sixth-placed finish at Troon in 1962.

In America, however, Snead was a consistent challenger when the major prizes were handed out. His third and final Masters title in 1954 pitted him against one of his greatest adversaries, Ben Hogan, in an 18-hole play-off. With a deft touch on the greens to compliment his high quality ball striking Snead defeated his illustrious opponent by one stroke. His three wins in the US PGA further underline just

how adept he was in head-to-head confrontations.

And yet for a player of such outstanding talent there remains a large gap in his impressive CV. Snead threw everything he had at the US Open but despite finishing in the top 10 on ten occasions (including four times as runner-up) he never won and the tournament became an albatross around his neck. The tone was set in 1937 when he made his US Open debut, finishing two shots behind Ralph Guldahl at Oakland Hills. Unfortunately for Snead, he would come even closer without winning in 1939. Needing a par-5 on the final hole at Spring Hill in Philadelphia to win he was caught in a greenside bunker before three putting and registering a triple bogey eight. Then, eight years later, he missed a putt of around 4ft to continue his play-off with Lew Worsham.

For all his natural ability, Snead was a temperamental player and many felt that in certain circumstances he lacked important tactical awareness. But the fact that he was an open character with tangible flaws doubtless contributed to his popularity. Snead was a rural boy, a hillbilly at heart, with such an attractive style that he inevitably drew comparisons with Bobby Jones.

Sam Snead died in 2002 as the most prolific winner the US Tour had ever seen. Dubbed, 'Slammin Sam' for his dynamic and powerful swing, he, above any other on this list, was perhaps blessed with the greatest God-given talent.

LEFT
Snead warms up for the Canada Cup in 1956, watched closely by his son.

FAR LEFT
Sam Snead accepts the Open trophy in 1946.

ANNIKA
SORENSTAM

Born: Stockholm, Sweden October 9, 1970

Turned professional: 1992

Kraft Nabisco Championship: Winner in 2001, 2002, 2005

LPGA Championship: Winner in 2003, 2004, 2005

US Women's Open: Winner in 1995, 1996

Du Maurier Classic/Women's British Open: Winner in 2003

Solheim cup record: Member of 7 European teams (1994, 1996, 1998, 2000, 2002, 2003, 2005). Played 27, Won 16, Lost 8, Halved 3

Annika Sorenstam is without question the greatest female golfer of the modern era. Just as Tiger Woods has dominated the men's game, Sorenstam has left a glorious legacy, a crucial chapter in the history of the women's game. To ally her deadly accurate ball striking she has the sort of mental strength that drives her game when under pressure and breathes fear into the hearts of those around her on the leaderboard. Her current tally of nine major championships, that includes victories in each of the big four, is an achievement that no other player in the modern era has come close to matching.

Annika Sorenstam was born into a sports-mad family in Stockholm in October 1970 but it was tennis, not golf, which received the lion's share of her attention growing up. Both Annika and her sister Charlotte reached a high standard within the junior ranks in Sweden but a weak backhand became a frustrating hurdle that Annika was unable to overcome and so she slowly began to devote more of her attention to golf. Under the guidance of Swedish coach Henri Reiss she developed the key fundamentals for a solid long game and, aged 19, travelled to America to enroll at the University of Arizona where she soon made her mark on the amateur game. In 1992 she played in the winning World Amateur Team Championships and realised a dream by qualifying for the US Open at Oakmont. It was the crowning moment in a glorious amateur career that inspired her to turn pro.

Annika Sorenstam took to life on Tour with ease and finished her rookie season in third place on the European Tour's Order of Merit. This initial success paved the way for her to take up membership of the USLPGA Tour in 1994 and a steady season was rewarded with a place on the European Solheim Cup team for the clash at The Greenbrier Golf Club in West Virginia. Sorenstam performed solidly in a losing team and announced herself on the international stage.

But her major breakthrough came in 1995. At the start of the US Tour season she

was a regular top 10 finisher and in June she travelled to Europe where she proceeded to win twice. Heading into the US Open at Broadmoor Golf Club in Colorado she was at the top of her game. A sparkling opening round 67 was followed by two scores in the 70s and Sorenstam found herself trailing Meg Mallon by five strokes going into the final day. But the 24-year-old shot a closing round of 68 to pile the pressure on her more experienced opponent. Mallon's game then crumbled under the heat, leaving her Swedish challenger one shot clear at the top of the leaderboard.

Sorenstam successfully defended her US Open crown in 1996 by a staggering eight shot margin, cementing her status as the dominant force within the women's game. But then, just as the Swede appeared to be in a class of her own, the major victories suddenly dried up. For five years she competed successfully on Tour without clinching any of the big four and Australian Karrie Webb emerged to take her crown as the number one golfer in the world.

In 2001 Annika Sorenstam realised that to fulfil her considerable potential she needed to dedicate herself to the game like she had done at the start of her career. A strict physical training regime was complimented by sheer hard work on the range and her results immediately picked up. On her way to victory at the Standard Register PING tournament she became the first female professional to

break 60 in competition and then returned to the major winner's circle with victory at the LPGA Nabisco Championship. She finished the 2001 season with eight victories and over two million dollars to her name.

Since then Sorenstam has won countless Tour titles and at least one major every year. Then, having scaled the heights of the women's game, she sought a brand new challenge in 2003 and by entering The Colonial tournament at Forth Worth became the first female to compete on the premier men's Tour since Babe Zaharis in 1945. Under intense media scrutiny she finished five over par and missed the cut but, despite failing to make the weekend, proved that her game was strong enough to take on the men.

Annika Sorenstam's record of nine major victories is the single most outstanding achievement in the women's game. Thirteen years after making her debut as a touring professional she still has an unwavering determination to add to her list of achievements. By the end of her career there will be a new benchmark against which all future superstars will be judged.

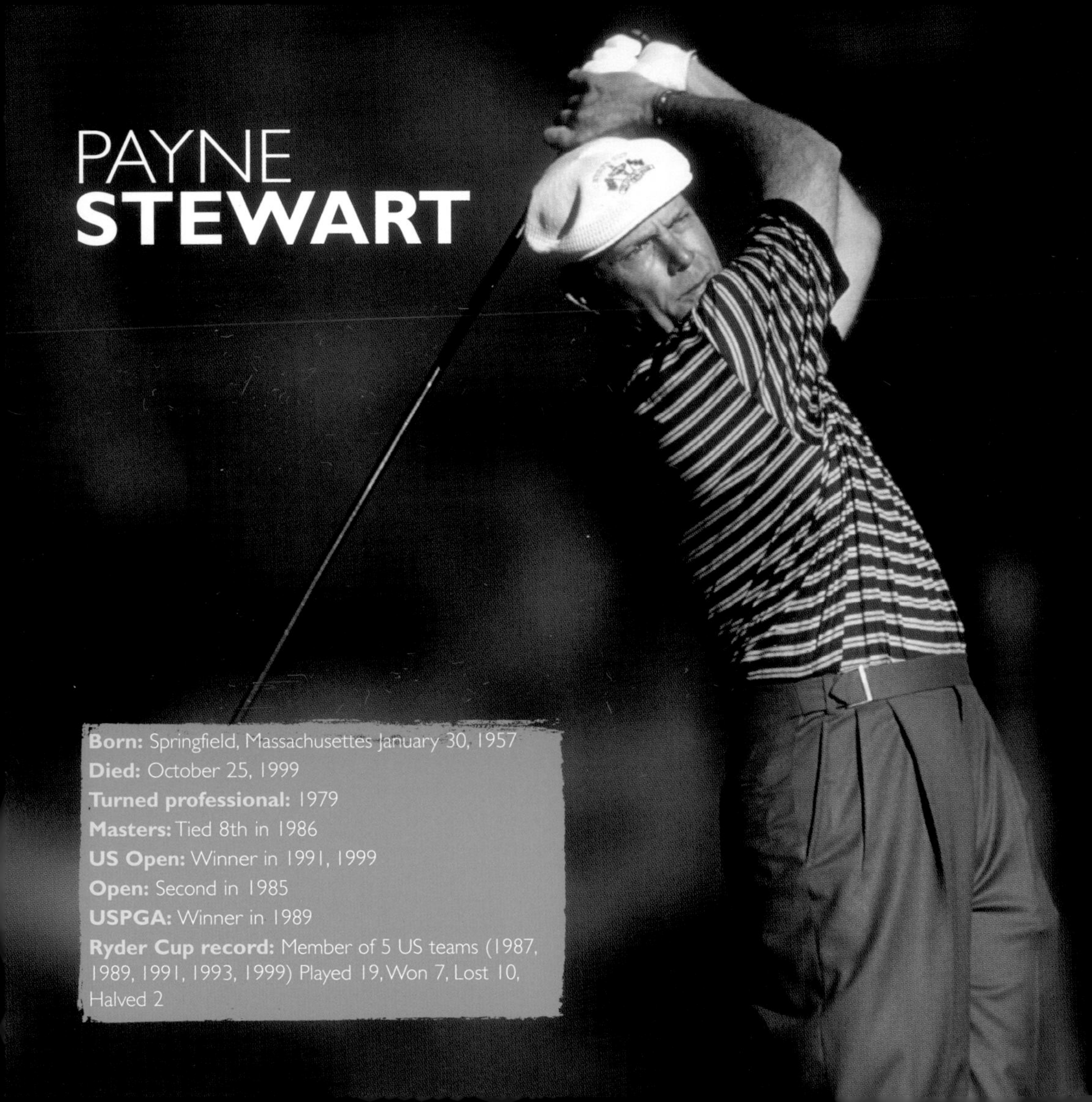

PAYNE
STEWART

Born: Springfield, Massachusettes January 30, 1957

Died: October 25, 1999

Turned professional: 1979

Masters: Tied 8th in 1986

US Open: Winner in 1991, 1999

Open: Second in 1985

USPGA: Winner in 1989

Ryder Cup record: Member of 5 US teams (1987, 1989, 1991, 1993, 1999) Played 19, Won 7, Lost 10, Halved 2

Dressed in plus fours, tam-o-shanter hat and psychedelic socks, Payne Stewart always cut the most recognisable figure on the golf course. His was a dashing game built on an elegance and style that justified his eye-catching outfits and endeared him to galleries around the world. His three major victories succeeded countless near misses as he learnt the art of winning through the pain of defeat. But Stewart never bemoaned bad luck and his genuine sportsmanship made him popular among his fellow professionals. When he died tragically in 1999, at the age of 42, the golfing world mourned the loss of one of its dearest sons.

BELOW
Stewart in Ryder Cup action, 1987.

Payne Stewart was introduced to the game at the age of four by his father Bill Stewart, an accomplished player in his own right who had won the Missouri State Amateur Championship and qualified to play in the 1955 US Open. Under Bill's guidance Payne developed as a serious player, earning a place on the South Methodist University golf team. But when he turned professional in 1979 he was far from the being the polished international performer that he later became. He chose to ply his trade on the Asian Tour where he learnt the art of building a score under pressure, and victories in India and Indonesia were crucial to financing his travels as well as his development as a golfer.

But after finally earning his playing privileges for the US Tour in 1982 Stewart developed an unwanted reputation as a choker. After narrow misses in the 1985 Opens of America and Britain he led with six holes to play at the 1986 Shinnecock Hills US Open but was outmuscled by the more experienced Ray Floyd. By this time his reputation as the best player never to have won a major preceded him. But he remained adamant that he had the mental strength to become a major winner and in 1989 captured the USPGA Championship at Kemper Lakes. The manner of this victory proved beyond doubt that he was a gritty fighter capable of producing his best golf just when he needed it the most. With nine holes left to

play Stewart sat five shots behind the leader, Mike Reid, but applied the pressure by making five birdies over the final seven holes for a spectacular back nine score of 31. Reid faltered during the closing stretch and Stewart became a major winner, aged 32.

Two years later at Hazeltine, Minnesota, he again made crucial birdies at the death to force a play-off with Scott Simpson for the US Open. The extra-time head-to-head was memorable as an exhibition of bitter determination by Stewart. His game had fragmented overnight and he was forced to rely on a deft touch around the greens, scraping together a score of 75 to beat Simpson by two.

Payne Stewart made five Ryder Cup appearances in total, winning seven matches and losing 10. After taking points in each of his five matches on debut in 1987 Stewart remained an ever present in the US team until 1993. But after the American team tasted victory at the Belfry Stewart's form dipped and he was forced to sit out the next two encounters. In 1999, after a spiritual awakening had encouraged him to re-dedicate himself to his family and his career, Stewart returned to form with a victory at the start of the season at Pebble Beach.

That year the US Open was held at Pinehurst, a narrow tree-lined course that places a premium on accurate ball striking and a patient gameplan. Over the last nine holes an exciting duel between Stewart and Phil Mickelson emerged. The damp and dingy conditions had made scoring tough and by keeping their scores intact Mickelson and Stewart had detached from the field. On the 17th tee there was nothing between them, although a precise 6-iron approach allowed Stewart to make a birdie and take a one shot lead. But a wayward drive on the par-4 18th

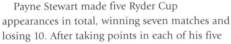

The Little Book of **GOLF** LEGENDS

forced him to lay up short of the green and a play-off seemed inevitable when his pitch finished 15ft from the pin. Payne Stewart proceeded to hole the longest ever putt to win the US Open.

This spectacular victory earned him a place on Ben Crenshaw's infamous 1999 Ryder Cup side at Brookline. Playing at the end of the singles field against Colin Montgomerie, Stewart performed an unprecedented act of sportsmanship. When it became clear that the US had won the cup Stewart conceded his match to the Scot who had faced a tirade of abuse from the crowd throughout the afternoon. On a

day when many American players damaged their reputations, Stewart showed a selfless disregard for his own record and had the integrity to put his own ambitions to one side.

Just one month after the clash at Brookline the golfing world was rocked as Stewart tragically died on board a learjet flying between Orlando and Texas. A gradual loss of cabin pressure was to blame for the hypoxia that killed everyone on board. After cruising on autopilot the plane finally ran out of fuel and crashed into a field in Aberdeen, South Dakota.

Payne Stewart's infectious character and striking wardrobe were responsible for injecting colour and sportsmanship into golf. His sudden death was a devastating blow that came at the end of a sparkling renaissance season in which he returned to the major winner's circle after an eight year hiatus.

JH**TAYLOR**

Born: Devon, England March 19, 1871
Died: February 10, 1963
Turned professional: 1890
US Open: 2nd in 1900
Open: Winner in 1894, 1895, 1900, 1909, 1913
Ryder Cup record: Captain in 1933

The youngest member of the "Great Triumvirate", John Henry Taylor was the first to make a serious breakthrough in the sport. His victory in the 1894 Open Championship at St. George's was the first by a player from outside Scotland. Building on this initial success he won the event on four more occasions and finished second a staggering five times. By his death in 1963 he had been a leading figure in the game, both on and off the course for almost a century.

BELOW
Taylor pictured in 1945.

JH Taylor was born and bred in the South West and by the age of 11 had started his golfing education by caddying for members at his local course in North Devon. As he watched accomplished golfers wrestling with this rugged links he learned that to build a decent score, especially in the wind, precise ball control was critical. As he began playing himself he developed a compact swing that squared the clubface regularly through impact. A solid technique led to some impressive performances and his reputation as a talented teenager grew quickly as he competed regularly for the Northam men's working club. At the age of 21 he secured a job as the first professional at Burnham and Berrow Golf Club in Somerset where he also fulfilled the role as greenkeeper.

The following year, Taylor showed his class by beating the respected St. Andrews professional Andrew Kirkaldy. As the Open at Prestwick loomed, JH Taylor was regarded as one of the field's most dangerous competitors despite never having experienced the unique pressure of the event. He duly confirmed his pre-tournament billing by shooting a record low 75 in the opening round but this was followed by a disappointing 89 in poor weather and Taylor's chances had all but gone. He eventually finished in a respectable, yet disappointing 10th place.

But Taylor would not have to wait long for the breakthrough he craved and in 1894 the Championship travelled south of the border for the first time to Sandwich in Kent. Taylor's shotmaking was too much for the rest of the field (he was the first

player to use lofted irons, like wedges, to attack greens) and his winning score of 326 was five shots better than Douglas Rolland in second. The first English venue provided the first English winner and JH Taylor had joined an elite group of players at golf's top table.

The following year Taylor showed his tenacity by recovering from an opening round 86 to remain in the hunt for the title. As the weather deteriorated through the final day the leader, Sandy Herd, faced St. Andrews at its meanest and Taylor emerged victorious by four strokes.

His second consecutive victory confirmed Taylor as the leading player of the time, but the emergence of Harry Vardon meant that he would have to wait five years before capturing his third Open crown.

In 1899 JH Taylor left his post at Burnham to take on the professional's job at Royal Mid Surrey, a course that was constructed under his guidance. Despite being an inland venue – close to London – Taylor was able to construct a course that reflected many of the traits that define and defend the challenge at Royal North Devon. Not a long course, Royal Mid Surrey still favours imaginative shotmakers able to negotiate a safe passage through the fierce rough and trees that line the fairways. Taylor remained the professional there until his retirement in 1946.

In the same year that Taylor joined Royal Mid Surrey he also crossed the Atlantic to play in the US Open. Not for the

first time, he finished second to Harry Vardon – the two taking their rivalry to an appreciative American crowd. The battle between them re-commenced later that year at St. Andrews and this time it was Taylor's turn to take the prize as he won his third Open title, beating Vardon by eight shots and James Braid by 13.

Between Taylor's first major triumph in 1894 and the start of World War I the "Great Triumvirate" dominated golf, providing the public with a fierce rivalry that served to raise the profile of the sport. Taylor prevailed in the Open on two more occasions in 1909 and 1913 and his other major achievements included winning the Matchplay Championship in 1908 and captaining the winning Great Britain and Ireland side in the 1933 Ryder Cup.

Like many of the great players featured in this book Taylor's impact stretched further than his achievements as a player. He became an accomplished course architect, lending his experienced eye to notable layouts such as Royal Birkdale and Machrihanish. He was also a major influence in the foundation of the Professional Golfers Association, an organisation that still works to uphold the interests of professional golfers. By the time he died at the age of 91, he had given back to the game just as much as he had taken.

PETER**THOMSON**

Born: Melbourne, Australia August 23, 1929
Turned professional: 1949
Masters: 5th in 1957
US Open: 4th 1956
Open: Winner in 1954, 1955, 1956, 1958, 1965

In 1954, Peter Thomson became the first Australian to win a major. He was an intelligent golfer with an acute strategic sense and a solid all-round game. In the heat of the battle Thompson would remain unfazed, focused on delivering the perfect shot at exactly the right moment. And it was this unique trait that marked him out as a player of supreme talent. Between 1952 and 1958 no British golfer finished above him in the Open and he won the Championship four times. When he added a fifth title in 1965, he confirmed his status as a true master of the links.

BELOW
Captain of the
Presidents Cup
International team
Peter Thomson, with
the trophy
in 1998.

The details of Peter Thomson's early career are somewhat sketchy but it is widely accepted that his initial intention was to become a chemist. When he finished as the top amateur in the Australian Open of 1948, however, it was clear that his future lay within golf. He turned pro in 1949 and, just like Bobby Locke 11 years before, Thompson made an immediate impact as a full-time player. He won the 1950 New Zealand Open and finished second in the Australian Open later that year. At this time a victory in Australasia would be worth far less than triumph in America but Thompson realised the need to prove himself at home – something he did in 1951 when he claimed the first of his three Australian Open titles.

It was not until 1953 that Thompson broadened his horizons and took to the States. He started a regular routine that would see him play in America during the early part of the season before returning to his homeland every July. Between 1953 and 1959, he had 42 top 10 finishes in America, including victory in the Texas Open and a fourth place finish in the US Open in 1956. The following year he finished fourth in the Masters but as Thompson reached his 30s, his trips to the States became more sporadic. For such a talented player, his limited success in America can be credited to the target golf style courses that place a premium on power off the tee and aggressive tactics. This was never the Australian's style and he

found himself more at home on the naturally crafted courses of the European Tour.

Peter Thomson and Bobby Locke may have been born on separate continents, 12 years apart, but their careers collided during a sparkling decade from 1949 in which they finished first or second in the Open twelve times. At the start of this period of dual dominance there was no doubt who was the more established player. Locke was a prolific winner on the US Tour and had also made his name in Europe. But Thompson's game was better suited to the unique challenge of the Open and he went one better than his South African counterpart by winning the Championship five times.

When the 1954 Open travelled to Royal Birkdale, Bobby Locke was bidding for his third title. Thompson was yet to make his mark but captured the Claret Jug by finishing one stroke ahead of the South African. Winning the Open and beating Locke in a tight head-to-head battle instilled the confidence in Thompson that kick-started his

domination of the event. His victories in the next two championships making him the first player to complete three consecutive wins since Bob Ferguson 74 years earlier.

Perhaps Thompson's greatest achievement, however, was his last Open triumph in 1965. Seven years after winning his fourth at St. Andrews, the 35-year-old was competing in a high quality field that included Arnold Palmer, Tony Lima and Jack Nicklaus. The Australian hung on to a slender two shot lead over Christie O'Connor with nerveless long iron approach shots to the final two greens. Throughout his Open career pressure seemed to draw the best from Thompson and this was no more apparent than at the death of the 1965 tournament.

His last major victory also served to silence critics in America who had questioned the calibre of the Open fields, struggling to understand how Thompson could be so prolific in Britain yet fail to make such an emphatic impact in the US. He again crushed any lingering American murmurs at the age of 55 when he won 10 times in one season on the US Seniors Tour.

Peter Thomson became the first Australian to reach the pinnacle of his profession. Dressed conservatively in dark clothes and white shoes he was a calm competitor who moved serenely around the course, unaffected by the pressure of crucial situations. His influence was to prove that Australian players had the ability to win at the highest level and the likes of Greg Norman, David Graham and Adam Scott have since continued this legacy.

LEFT
Peter Thomson along with Mark Calcavecchia, Sandy Lyle and Mark O'Meara in the Champions Challenge at St. Andrews in 2000.

FAR LEFT
Thompson on the practice ground at the Open, Royal Birkdale 1965.

LEE
TREVINO

Born: Dallas, Texas December 1, 1939
Turned professional: 1960
Masters: 10th in 1975
US Open: Winner in 1968, 1971
Open: Winner in 1971, 1972
USPGA: Winner in 1974, 1984
Ryder Cup record: Member of 6 US teams
(1969, 1971, 1973, 1975, 1979, 1981). Played 30,
Won 17, Lost 7, Halved 6. Captain in 1985

It is impossible to talk about Lee Trevino without emphasising the financial difficulties that punctuated his formative years. Many of the players featured in this book, such as Ben Hogan, Sam Snead and Gene Sarazen, rose to prominence from underprivileged beginnings but for Trevino golf was a means to scrape a few essential dollars to survive. As a hustler he developed a confident, talkative style that remained part of his infectious character throughout his career. With six majors and over 25 tour events to his name Trevino was the confident kid with a quirky swing who charmed knowledgeable audiences around the world.

BELOW
Trevino is all smiles after winning the Senior Legends of Golf Championship in 1996.

Lee Trevino was born into a fragmenting family in Dallas in 1939. Before he was old enough to remember his father walked out, leaving his Mexican mother and grandfather responsible for his upbringing. Money was a perpetual problem and before he was 10 years old Trevino would skip school to work in cotton fields to supplement the meagre family income. His schooling had finished altogether by the age of 14 as the need for cash exceeded the importance of gaining a comprehensive education. He took a job at a local driving range and it was here that his unlikely association with the game began. As an energetic teenager he would play whenever possible, and without anyone to guide him towards a mechanically sound technique he developed his own unique style.

When he reached the age of 17 Trevino opted for a secure income with the US Marines and served for four years. He was able to play, albeit sporadically, through this period and when he finished his tour of duty found a job as an assistant professional at a small club on the Mexican-American border.

Throughout Trevino's formative years he would take on any player willing to accept a challenge, regularly betting money that he simply didn't have on the outcome of a match against an opponent he barely knew. He was forced to back his talent and developed a ruthless mental streak to ally his natural ability that made him almost

impossible to defeat. To entice sceptical punters into lucrative wagers he would often play using a strange device fashioned from insulating tape and a Coke bottle. He gambled on his talent, inadvertently developing his game for the pressure of tournament golf.

In 1965 Trevino won the Texas State Open and the following year he qualified to play in the US Open. These achievements proved that a career playing golf could be lucrative, despite finishing way down the field in his first major appearance, Trevino clearly enjoyed his taste of golf at the highest level. In 1967 he returned to play in the same event at Baltusrol. Jack Nicklaus took the title but Trevino finished fifth and walked away with a cheque for $6,000. He loved the attention, valued the reward and took confidence from the knowledge that his game was fit for major golf.

"Supermex" won his first US Open in 1968 at Rochester in New York. Heading into the final round he trailed Bert Yancey by one stroke, but as Yancey struggled under the pressure so Trevino excelled, shooting 69 for the last 18 holes. Yancey's classic swing failed to stand up to Trevino's homemade version and the Mexican-American announced himself to the world in style, becoming the first winner of the US Open to complete all four rounds in the 60s. Furthermore, his ability to engage

the crowd with amusing banter throughout the week endeared him to the public.

Trevino's second US Open victory in 1971, at Merion, pitted him against Jack Nicklaus in a tense play-off. Proving that he feared none of his more accomplished rivals, Trevino shot 69 to Nicklaus's 71. He soon added the British Open to his US crown, revealing that his game was strong enough to prevail on a variety of contrasting layouts.

Perhaps his most famous win though was the Open of 1972 at Muirfield. As the reigning champion he arrived on the East Lothian coast among the favourites to win. After three rounds the diminutive Mexican was closely pursued by Jack Nicklaus and Tony Jacklin. When asked about how he would respond to the unique pressure of the situation Trevino famously told his interviewer, "try playing a hustler for $50 when you've only got $10 in your hip pocket. That's pressure." He proceeded to shoot a closing round 71 that included a chip in on the 17th to steal the momentum away from his English challenger.

Lee Trevino's career at the top level spanned three decades – his final major victory coming at the USPGA of 1984. His lively banter and ungainly swing contradicted the clinical strategy that made him such a consistent competitor and he played with a desperate desire to succeed that was always hidden beneath a disarming smile. Trevino's considerable achievements were a triumph of sheer natural talent emerging through an under-privileged background to scale the heights of the golfing world.

HARRY
VARDON

Born: Grouville, Jersey May 9, 1870
Died: March 20, 1937
Turned professional: 1890
Open: Winner in 1896, 1898, 1899, 1903, 1911, 1914
US Open: Winner in 1900

Born in Jersey in 1870, Harry Vardon was the most successful member of "The Great Triumvirate". While James Braid and JH Taylor both won the Open five times, Vardon went one better and his record six remains unequalled today. He was also a truly international competitor, travelling three times to America to play in, and win, countless exhibition and challenge matches as well as the US Open. These remarkable achievements seem even more spectacular when you consider that Vardon suffered a debilitating illness for much of his adult life.

BELOW
A portrait of Harry Vardon, 1904.

Unlike many of the great champions of the time, Vardon was certainly not destined to become a professional golfer. In fact it was not until 1877 that Jersey had a golf course, a project undertaken by a band of English visitors who designed a few holes near the Vardon family home. His father was a gardener and Harry himself had an array of different jobs through his early years – he worked on a dairy farm, assisted a doctor and served as a member of staff to a wealthy local Mayor. Indeed, it was Mayor Spofford of Beauview who encouraged Vardon's interest in the game, doubtless providing him with balls and clubs with which to play. Vardon left Jersey to take up the post as assistant professional at St. Annes in Lancashire and later moved to Studley Park where he was employed as both the professional and the greenkeeper.

Harry Vardon's early involvement in the game was purely as a means to make money, he did not compete very often and his brother Tom was regarded as the better player. But by 1894, Vardon's own game had reached a level that enabled him to compete in the Open at Sandwich. His creditable tie for fifth offered a glimpse of his talent.

In 1896 the Open was held at Muirfield and JH Taylor was looking to emulate Young Tom Morris's achievement of winning the Open three years in a row. Earlier in the season Taylor and Vardon had gone head-to-head in a challenge match and Vardon emerged victorious,

winning comprehensively by 8 and 6. So despite leading Vardon by six shots at the half way stage, Taylor knew what his talented opponent was capable of. Vardon slowly chipped away at Taylor's lead and after 72 holes the two were level. Vardon won the insuing 36-hole play-off convincingly by four shots. He was a worthy champion.

Having made this breakthrough, Vardon's self-confidence grew and he proceeded to win the Open twice more before the turn of the century. By this time he was an established star at the top of his game, ready to take on new challenges.

In 1900, he crossed the Atlantic to embark on an extensive tour of the States that took him from New England to Florida, the highlight of which was the US Open in Chicago. He proved that the standard of British golf was high by taking the title by a staggering nine stroke margin. But despite this glorious achievement, Vardon's trip to the US was a bittersweet experience. He returned to the UK exhausted, physically weakened and from this time to his death in 1937 serious health problems including tuberculosis, meant that he frequently required hospital treatment. After winning the 1903 Open at Prestwick, where serious physical fatigue almost put a premature end to his challenge, he was

admitted to a local sanatorium.

Vardon's next major victory came again in the Open Championship, eight years later. His final Open triumph in 1914 marked an end to the dominance of "The Great Triumvirate". Between them Vardon, Taylor and Braid had won the event 16 times in 20 years, their fierce rivalry and great skill had gone a long way to increase public interest in the sport.

LEFT
Vardon chips from the rough, 1924.

FAR LEFT
Vardon at the Open in 1920.

Harry Vardon had also played a crucial role in the increasing popularity of the game in the US. In 1913 he returned to America to compete in the now legendary US Open at Brookline, near Boston. At the half way stage Vardon held a healthy two shot lead over fellow Jersey islander Ted Ray and was four ahead of the amateur, Francis Ouimet. Completing the last seven holes in an awesome 26 shots, Ouimet managed to force a play-off with his two revered opponents. His one over par score of 72 for the 18 holes that ensued was five better than Vardon and six better than Ray. Despite losing this epic contest, Vardon had played his part in a dramatic passage of play that has since gone down in golfing folklore, capturing the imagination of the American people.

Harry Vardon was a student of the game, he developed his own theory about how to hold and swing the club that broke tried and tested methods. He realised the importance of making his hands work together – although not the first to use it, he certainly popularised the overlapping grip that has since been dubbed 'The Vardon Grip'. His swing was fluid and more upright than his contemporaries with an aesthetic beauty that was fresh and far more reminiscent of what we see today.

TOM
WATSON

Born: Kansas City, Missouri September 4, 1949
Turned professional: 1971
Masters: Winner in 1977, 1981
US Open: Winner in 1982
Open: Winner in 1975, 1977, 1980, 1982, 1983
USPGA: Tied 2nd in 1978
Ryder Cup record: Member of 4 US teams
(1977, 1981, 1983, 1989). Played 15, Won 10, Lost 4,
Halved 1. Captain in 1993

With a dynamic swing and aggressive strategy Tom Watson captivated audiences all around the world, emerging through a golden period in the game's history with eight majors to his name. His powerful yet compact swing was tailor made for the links and his achievements in our Open Championship are a monument to his masterful manipulation of the golf ball.

BELOW
Watson in the Buick Invitational, 1992 tournament.

Despite not having a legacy of golf within the family Tom Watson's route into the professional ranks was fairly smooth. His father was a successful insurance broker and the Watson family enjoyed a comfortable living in Kansas City, Missouri. This enabled him to play golf at the nearby Prairie Dunes Country Club, where he developed an early infatuation with the game. After completing high school he enrolled at Stanford University to study psychology, marrying his academic and golfing education with success. By the age of 21, and with a handful of amateur titles under his belt, he then embarked on a career as a touring professional.

Tom Watson emerged through a successful American university system that continues to deliver high quality golfers to the Tour. However, his first few seasons were tough as he pitted his game against far more experienced players. Evidence of his immaturity at the highest level was seen at the US Open of 1974 when he entered the final round one shot ahead of Hale Irwin. The pressure of the situation and the severity of the challenge at Winged Foot proved too much for the 25-year-old and he shot a final round 79. Under the glare of an expectant American public his game had fallen to pieces and Watson quickly developed a reputation as a choker.

He underlined his obvious talent however by winning the Western Open later that year and this first US Tour victory was the springboard for his emphatic arrival to the major winners' circle in 1975. The venue was Carnoustie on Scotland's east coast – a notoriously difficult layout – and Watson was making his Open debut.

He was far better equipped to handle the pressure of the closing stages than the previous year and emerged to win a tight play-off against Australian Jack Newton by a single shot. Watson had triumphed at the Open on his first attempt, without even completing a full practice round, and it was clear that his game was suited to the links.

Two years later he won his first Green Jacket, narrowly defeating Jack Nicklaus by two shots. Their fierce but friendly rivalry was to be the star attraction when battle re-commenced that summer at Turnberry for the Open where a rare heatwave had parched the course. The hard, fast fairways and equally slick greens made for a low scoring Championship and in a barrage of birdies Watson and Nicklaus rose to the head of the field. Entering the final round the pair were tied after both had shot rounds of 68, 70 and 65. They sustained the birdie rush through the final afternoon, accelerating away from the field. Standing all square on the par 5 17th tee, Watson followed a long drive with a precise second into the heart of the green and two putted for a birdie. Nicklaus, however, came up short in two, chipped and two putted for a par. With a slender one-shot lead Watson split the final fairway with a supremely struck 1-iron. Nicklaus was forced to attack at all costs and pushed his drive, narrowly

avoiding a bush to the right of the fairway. From there Nicklaus found the green, albeit 30ft from the hole, and the pressure was back on Watson who responded with a sparkling 7-iron to 25ins. In one last twist Nicklaus holed his 30 footer, forcing Watson to make his short putt for the title. He duly did so and the 'duel in the sun', as it became known, remains one of the greatest final round battles of all time.

LEFT
Watson alongside Jack Nicklaus checks the run of the green at the Open, Turnberry, 1977.

FAR LEFT
Tom Watson with the Claret Jug in 1982.

Watson won the Open again in 1980 at Muirfield, before claiming his only US Open victory in 1982. The venue was Pebble Beach and once again it was Jack Nicklaus applying the pressure. The two were tied on the par-3 17th but Watson was in dire straits having pulled his tee shot into deep rough to the left of the green. Remarkably, he holed his recovery shot and again defeated Nicklaus by a single stroke.

Back-to-back victories in 1982 and 1983 made it five Open crowns for Watson, equalling the achievements of J H Taylor and James Braid, and in 1984 he came within touching distance of Harry Vardon's super six. But a wayward approach to the St. Andrews road hole in the final round, and an inspired performance by a 27-year-old Seve Ballesteros, conspired against Watson and Vardon's record remained in tact.

Tom Watson's achievements seem even more remarkable when you consider the calibre of the players he consistently beat. From Trevino and Nicklaus to Ballesteros and Faldo, Watson proved that aggressive, exciting golf could be a successful formula. He was a modern day master of the links who still holds a special place in the hearts of British golf fans.

TIGER
WOODS

Born: Cypress, California December 30, 1975
Turned professional: 1996
Masters: Winner in 1997, 2001, 2002, 2005
US Open: Winner in 2000, 2002,
Open: Winner in 2000, 2005, 2006
USPGA: Winner in 1999, 2000, 2006
Ryder Cup record: Member of 5 US teams
(1997, 1999, 2002, 2004). Played 25, Won 10, Lost 13,
Halved 2

For Tiger Woods to be universally recognised as the greatest golfer to have lived he will have to surpass Jack Nicklaus's record of 18 major victories. This remains the only milestone of any serious significance untouched by a man whose phenomenal natural talent, physical might and psychological strength have swept his peers mercilessly aside. His athletic yet smooth style coupled with his ruthless and successful pursuit of glory have made him a multi-million dollar commercial asset like no golfer before him. His presence in the field single-handedly raises the profile of any event, guaranteeing international audiences and vast galleries. The world now waits with baited breath to see just how far Tiger Woods can go.

Looking closely at his upbringing, it would appear that Tiger Woods was destined to become a top-flight golfer. Even as early as six months old, he would mimic his father's golf swing and by the age of three he had a score of 48 for nine holes and a television appearance in which he putted alongside Bob Hope under his belt.

The crucial influence in Tiger's early attraction to the game was undoubtedly his father. Earl Woods had served as a lieutenant colonel in the US Army and was quick to spot and nurture his son's talent. (Indeed, it was Earl who gave his son the nickname Tiger after a close military friend of the same title.) As a junior, Tiger's phenomenal talent was clear from the start. He became the youngest ever winner of the US Junior Championship,

aged just 15 and the following year he was good enough to warrant a place in his first professional event, the Nissan Los Angeles Open. In 1994, he enrolled at Stanford University, where his game developed under a structured coaching regime. Competing at University enabled Woods to pit his game against many of the world's best amateurs – he won 10 collegiate events and earned a place in the 1995 Walker Cup. After capturing his third consecutive US Amateur title in 1996 it was clear that having conquered the amateur world Tiger Woods was ready for life on Tour.

BELOW
Woods in action at the Players Championship Sawgrass, 2000.

His decision to turn pro in August 1996 left just seven events to secure his playing privileges for the following year. Remarkably, he won twice and finished in the top 10 three times to propel himself to 25th place on the moneylist. In a career littered with glory, this remains one of his finest achievements.

Tiger's first major triumph came at the US Masters in 1997 but after the opening nine holes he appeared to have blown his chances with a disastrous four over par score of 40. From the 10th tee his form returned spectacularly – he shot 30 for the inward half and followed his opening round of 70 with scores of 66, 65 and 69. At 21, he became the youngest ever Masters champion and his staggering 12-shot winning margin was a new record. It was a performance built on power and control, proving that Woods was a cut above the best players on the planet. He quickly added to this success and by mid-June 1997, the world had a new number one golfer. Still just 21, Tiger Woods became the youngest man to reach this milestone.

His finest season to date however was in 2000. The first of his three major victories arrived at Pebble Beach in the US Open. In wet and windy conditions, the field struggled to tame a course set up by the USGA to push the best players in the world to the limit. Woods laid on a masterclass that was virtually perfect in every department of the game. He finished the event on 12 under par – no other player managed to break into red figures. His 15-stroke winning margin smashed the previous record of 13 set by Old Tom Morris, 138 years

earlier. Many believe this to be the finest strokeplay performance in the history of the sport.

Woods maintained this level of performance to capture the two remaining majors in 2000 and become the youngest player to win each of the big four. Then when he took the 2001 Masters, he became the only golfer ever to hold all four majors simultaneously.

During this period of supremacy few would have questioned that they were watching the most talented golfer of all time. But through 2003 and 2004 Tiger failed to win a single major. Having parted company with his coach, Butch Harmon, Woods decided to regulate his swing by himself. From the outside this looked a strange decision and his form duly dipped. Vijay Singh muscled in to take his world number one spot in September 2004 and Tiger lost his air of invincibility. As frustrating as it was for Woods, media criticism of his decision to part with Harmon was inevitable. Each week on Tour his technique was pulled apart by former player's attempting to explain why Tiger was unable to tame his driver. At the start of 2004, Woods employed the services of swing-guru, Hank Haney and the adjustments the two made paid off as Tiger returned to his imperious best by winning the Masters and Open in 2005.

With 10 majors already to his name, it might seem strange to say it but Tiger Woods is entering a critical phase in his career. If he is to stand proudly as the finest golfer of all time he will need to march on relentlessly through his 30s. But regardless of whether he reaches Jack Nicklaus's record or not, it will be a journey that no true golf fan will want to miss.

FAR LEFT
Tiger Woods in the Masters play-off 2005, celebrates sinking a putt on his way to the title.

LEFT
Woods on the final tee of the 2005 Open, in which he secured victory.

BELOW
Woods with the 1999 USPGA trophy.

The Little Book of
CRICKET
LEGENDS
RALPH**DELLOR** and STEPHEN**LAMB**

The Little Book of
FOOTBALL
LEGENDS
GRAHAM**BETTS**

The Little Book of
GRAND PRIX
LEGENDS
PHILIP**RABY**

The Little Book of
RUGBY
LEGENDS
PAUL**MORGAN** and ALEX**MEAD**

THE PICTURES IN THIS BOOK WERE PROVIDED COURTESY OF THE FOLLOWING:

GETTY**IMAGES**
101 Bayham Street, London NW1 0AG

EMPICS
www.empics.com

PHIL**SHELDON**GOLF**PICTURE**LIBRARY
40 Manor Way, Barnet, Hertfordshire EN5 2JQ

Concept and Art Direction:
VANESSA **and** KEVIN**GARDNER**

Design and Artwork: KEVIN**GARDNER**

Image research: ELLIE**CHARLESTON**

PUBLISHED BY GREEN UMBRELLA PUBLISHING

Publishers:
JULES**GAMMOND and** VANESSA**GARDNER**

Series Editor: VANESSA**GARDNER**

Written by: NEIL**TAPPIN**